EVERYDAY SCIENCE

66
experiments that explain the small and big things all around us

BARRON'S

Contents

Geology experiments

Physics experiments

Chemistry experiments

Biology experiments

Science in your backpack

Watch your step!

The ground beneath our feet is the uppermost layer of the earth's crust and has formed as a result of physical and chemical changes brought about by creatures who live on it (such as ourselves). While there are many different types of terrain, they are composed of the same basic components—decomposed organic material, minerals, and fragments of rock of different sizes. These rocks are also from the earth's crust but have often traveled very far from their point of origin. Each type of terrain contains different layers of material.

What will you need?

- A shovel
- Gardening gloves
- A journal
- A pencil
- A permanent marker pen
- A magnifying glass
- Measuring tape or ruler
- Plastic bags or small jars (plastic or glass)

Experiment

Would you like to excavate and find out what is buried under your feet? In some places the ground has developed to a degree where you can distinguish up to five separate horizontal layers.

1
Find a place where you can dig a hole 24 inches (60 cm) in diameter and 24 inches (60 cm) deep.

2
Start to excavate, observing how the color of the earth changes the deeper you dig down. Every color indicates a layer; measure the height of these horizontal bands and make a note in your jounal.

3
Examine the type of material in each layer, as well as their color. You might not find all five layers where you dig, so don't worry if you can't find one or two of them!

THINK LIKE A SCIENTIST

The different layers that you have described have their own names and characteristics. You can easily identify them from this short checklist:

HUMUS. This upper layer consists of fallen leaves and other organic matter that can still be identified, while organic matter in the lower section is decomposed plants that can no longer be identified as such.

"A" HORIZON. Organic material and minerals. It is normally dark gray (almost black) but can be lighter in color if it contains less organic matter.

"B" HORIZON. This layer is an accumulation of clays and substances that water has dissolved and permeated through "A" Horizon.

"C" HORIZON. Rock that has been weathered and fragmented. This layer is soft and easy to dig through.

"D" HORIZON. Hard to dig through as it consists of a high density of larger rock fragments (this layer is often called "bedrock").

Continue investigating

You can widen your study by identifying and noting down the characteristics of each layer that you have excavated and stored. Use the tip of a pencil to separate the different components, and examine them with a magnifying glass. If you want to know if your samples contain minerals, use a magnet. Use the granulometry table on p. 37 to describe and measure the materials that you have recovered.

Needle in a haystack

Sometimes it is necessary to find something buried somewhere underground in a large area, but it would be impossible to dig the whole area up. The Georadar is an instrument that sends and receives electromagnetic waves, identifying underground elements and characteristics such as mineral deposits, bones, mineshafts, buried munitions, swords, and other weapons to be excavated.

4 Write down if the soil is claylike, sandy, or full of rock fragments. Also record the presence or remains of living organisms (earthworms, snails, insects, fungi, plant and tree roots, dead leaves...).

5 Take a small sample of earth from each layer and store them in your plastic bags or jars so that you can look at them at home later under a magnifying glass. Don't forget to clearly label your samples so that you will know which is which later on! Draw pictures in your journal.

The time machine

If it is night and you are high in the mountains, far from the lights of the big city, you can see many, many stars. You are in fact seeing them as people would have many years ago. We see some stars as they existed millions of years ago, when dinosaurs roamed the earth!

If you are between eight and eleven years old, you are in luck; some stars you can see are exactly the same as they were when you were born. Would you like to know which stars they are?

What will you need?

- To be in a place far from light and big cities
- A moonless night
- Warm clothes
- A planisphere (you can find this on the Internet and print it out)
- A compass

Experiment

Are you ready to travel through time?

1

If you are eight or nine and live in the northern hemisphere, look for the star Sirius. Go outside on a January evening around midnight and face south. Sirius is the brightest star in the sky. You will find it just two or three palm lengths (with your arm outstretched) from the horizon. You are seeing the star as it was eight-and-a-half years ago.

2

If you are 10 or 11, find Sirius and then stretch up with both of your arms and measure one palm to the left. You will see another very bright star called Procyon. The light reaching your eyes from this star began its journey 10-and-a-half years ago, when you were born!

3

If you live in the southern hemisphere, you can find Sirius during the month of March between 10 and 11 o'clock at night. Look to the east, close to the horizon.

THINK LIKE A SCIENTIST

Why do you think the stars appear as they were a long time ago?

Are all the stars the same distance away from us?

Everything that we see, we see because its light reaches us. Some objects, such as this book, the moon, and other planets, reflect light. Others, such as light bulbs, our sun, and all the other stars, emit their own light. This light takes time to reach us; for example, while the light from this book takes an insignificant fraction of a second to reach us, and the light from the sun takes eight minutes… the light from the nearest star, Alpha Centauri, takes four years to arrive! This means that we are seeing Alpha Centauri as it was four years ago. If we could make a very, very powerful telescope, we could see what the inhabitants of planets around Alpha Centauri were doing; it would be like having a time machine, as we could see what they were doing four years ago, not what they are doing right now.

The further away a star is, the more time it takes for its light to reach our eyes. There are stars that are 10 light years away (this means that the light left them 10 years ago), 100 light years away, and millions of light years away.

Continue investigating

Take your planisphere outside on a clear, star-filled night to take a good look and learn a bit about the brightest constellations. If you are in the Earth's northern hemisphere, look for Ursa Major, which forms part of Orion, a constellation with three stars in a line, or the Polar Star, which magically always tells us which direction is north.

If you are in the southern hemisphere, look for the Southern Cross that always points toward the south. You will also find the constellations of Musca and Centauri, where we find the star closest to the earth in the whole universe: Alpha Centauri!

The furthest galaxy

The furthest heavenly body a telescope can observe is galaxy z8_GND_5296, at no less than 13,100 million light years distant. It was discovered in 2013 by the Keck I telescope in Hawaii. The light that reaches this telescope has been traveling from its stars for 13,100 million years, when our universe was only 700 million years old. Neither our Earth nor the sun even existed that long ago!

4

In the southern hemisphere on the same night, Procyon will be the brightest star, only a few palms to the right of Sirius.

Baby galaxies

Astronomers use this time machine effect to study what galaxies looked like thousands of millions of years ago, when the universe had just been born and there were still "baby galaxies." By doing this, they can investigate what the universe was like all that time ago, just after its birth. These galaxies are very far—thousands of millions of light years away from us. That is why we have to use huge telescopes to properly observe them.

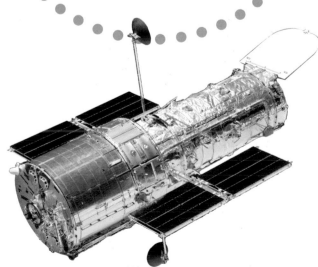

The history detective

Next time you go on a trip to the mountains, look closely at the rocks and stones all around you. Some are white and hide a surprising past: they are the remains of skeletons of small shellfish and coral that lived on the bottom of the ocean millions of years ago. But not all of the white rocks that you will find have such a spectacular history. Did you know that with a simple experiment, you can find out if the rock you are walking on once formed part of a beautiful coral reef?

What will you need?

- White- or light-colored stones, gathered from different places
- Transparent beakers
- White vinegar
- Plastic bags

Experiment

Do you want to become a true history detective?

1
While you're out walking in the mountains, keep an eye out for outcrops of white- or light-colored rocks.

2
Take a small sample of each type of rock—any small stone that you can easily take away with you.

3
Once you're at home, fill as many transparent beakers with white vinegar as stones you have collected.

THINK LIKE A SCIENTIST

Why do bubbles form on the outside of the stones?

These rocks are made of a chemical compound called calcium carbonate, which reacts to acid, such as the acid in the vinegar. They release a gas: carbon dioxide. You can see how this gas forms the bubbles that appear all over the stones.

These calcareous or limestone rocks were formed millions of years ago, when the shells of thousands and thousands of small marine creatures living on coral reefs at the bottom of the sea were crushed together. The area that you were walking on was once underwater!

Continue investigating

Try this experiment with another acid: lemon juice. Although the effect is often less spectacular, you can also observe bubbles of carbon dioxide coming out from rocks that contain calcium carbonate.

Shilin forest

Some limestone rocks form spectacular vistas as water dissolves them over thousands and thousands of years. Surely you have one nearby worth visiting. The Shilin forest in China looks like something out of a fairy tale!

4 Place the stones carefully into the beakers and watch what happens.

5 In some beakers you will see bubbles form on the outside of the stones. When this happens, you can be sure that these rocks are made from animals that lived in a prehistoric ocean!

6 But sometimes you won't see any bubbles. You've probably picked up a piece of sandstone, a "fossil" of a prehistoric beach... or maybe granite, quartzite, or another mineral.

GRANITE

QUARTZITE

OTHER

Caught you!

We can construct a trap for nocturnal insects in order to observe the huge diversity of life in our forests at night. Unfurl your sheet and keep your eyes peeled!

What will you need?

- A white sheet
- A white spotlight
- String
- Clothespins
- A camera
- A book to help you identify insects

Experiment

What kind of bugs flit through our forests at night?

1

Tie the string between two trees, parallel to the ground.

2

Hang the sheet over the string and fix it in place with the clothespins, as if you were hanging it out to dry. You could also keep it straight by weighing the bottom down with stones.

3

Place a white spotlight behind the sheet.

THINK LIKE A SCIENTIST

Why do you think that the insects are attracted by the light?

What type of insect trap do you think you could use during daylight?

Some insects are attracted to natural light because they use it to characterize their behavior. The moon serves them as a point of reference in the darkness. Phototaxis is a phenomenon that explains why some insects are attracted to the light while others are not. Some insects (such as cockroaches) have negative phototaxis and flee from light. Others (such as flies) have positive phototaxis and are attracted by light.

Diurnal insects use smells rather than natural light as a point of reference. In fact, they communicate through pheromones, airborne substances that they secrete to attract members of the opposite sex. We humans use pest control methods based on these pheromones, meaning that they are not dangerous to plants or other insects.

Continue investigating

Pheromones are a sex hormone that butterflies secrete to communicate with each other. This method of communication allows a widely dispersed species to communicate over large distances; for example, the giant peacock moth can detect pheromones up to 12.4 miles (20 km) away. Insects detect the presence of pheromones with the antennae, explaining the complex structure of this delicate apparatus.

Lethal phototaxis

Not all animals can see the same type of light that we do. For example, we cannot see ultraviolet light (or black light) or the infrared radiation that animals can see. Many types of insects are naturally drawn by ultraviolet radiation, and for this reason we manufacture UV lights surrounded by an electric grill. These kill harmful or bothersome insects, such as mosquitoes and flies, by attracting them with their irresistible light.

4

When the sun goes down, get ready to receive your visitors! Your light trap will not harm the insects. We recommend that you take photographs of all of the different species so that you can easily identify them later!

Traveling insects

It is becoming more and more common to find insect species native to other countries on our own doorstep. While they are unable to cover such huge distances themselves, they may have hitched a ride on goods being transported by plane or boat. For example, the tiger mosquito originated in southeast Asia but is now spreading over other continents thanks to human enterprise. It is much more aggressive than the common mosquito; it is active throughout the day, and its bites are much more painful.

Another notable example is the red palm weevil or palm weevil, native to tropical Asia. As a result of human intervention, it has now spread to Africa, America, and Europe, where it is destroying both indigenous and ornamental palm species.

Total protection

Soil erosion is a part of the life cycle of rocks, but it can be problematic in rural areas, where many people depend on the land for their livelihood. This simple experiment will demonstrate how important vegetation is to prevent soil erosion and the subsequent loss of nutrients.

What will you need?

- 2 deep trays, about 12 inches (30 cm) x 6 inches (15 cm)
- Enough soil to fill half of each tray
- A square of turf or quick-growing grass seeds
- 2 pieces of wood the same width as the trays
- 2 supports (for example, wooden blocks or stones)
- A garden trowel (if you need to cut a square of grass from a lawn)
- Water
- Watering can or container with holes in the bottom

Experiment

Follow these four steps and you will be able to investigate how vegetation cover protects soil against erosion by heavy rain.

1 Equally angle two identical trays over the supports.

2 Fill each tray halfway with the same type of soil. You can prevent the soil from slipping down by using a piece of wood to hold it in place.

3 Cover the soil in one of the trays with a thin layer of grass (you can take this from the garden with a trowel or buy it from a gardening shop), leaving the soil in the other tray free of vegetation.

THINK LIKE A SCIENTIST

Which tray accumulates more muddy water at the bottom? Where does this mud come from? The water percolates through the contents of the grass tray almost intact, without removing sediments or nutrients and emerging crystal clear at the bottom. In the tray without vegetation, water is murky because it has dragged through nutrients—this is how soil erosion takes place, and the result is sterile and eroded soil.

Vegetation plays an important role in protecting soil from the direct impact of raindrops, regulating their flow to the surface, which in turn strengthens its roots and prevents erosion.

Continue investigating

Terrain that is subject to strong winds and has little vegetation cover can be stripped of soil particles, degrading the quality of soil and decreasing agricultural productivity. You can test this by gathering soil samples, placing them in a tray, and directing an electric fan on them for a given period of time. Before you begin, ensure that your soil samples are dry, as damp samples will not allow you to observe the effect of the wind on them. Which sample has suffered less wind erosion?

Straw protection

After a series of destructive wildfires in Galicia (Spain) in the summer of 2013, experts and investigators devised a plan to protect soil without vegetation cover from erosion and flooding. They delivered payloads of wheat straw via helicopter, a technique known as air mulching.

A strange word: gorge

Gorges are deep, wide furrows formed when torrential rain erodes soft rock (principally sandstones and clays) in areas with little or no vegetation. They typically occur in semidesert areas such as Texas, New Mexico, and Arizona. You have surely seen them in Western movies!

4

Use a watering can (or a container with holes in the bottom) to soak both trays over the course of a few weeks, until the water begins to gather below the soil line. Note the color of the water that gathers in each tray.

I'm melting with cold!

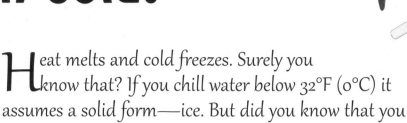

Heat melts and cold freezes. Surely you know that? If you chill water below 32°F (0°C) it assumes a solid form—ice. But did you know that you can melt ice and snow below 32°F (0°C)?

What will you need?

- A glass
- Crushed ice or frost from freezer
- Tablespoon
- Salt
- A thermometer that can measure below 32°F (0°C)

Experiment

Do you want to see how to "melt with cold"?

1
Fill a glass full of snow or crushed ice. You can find snow in your own house by scraping a plastic or wooden spoon across the frost in your freezer compartment.

2
Put the thermometer into the glass so that it comes into contact with the ice. Wait a few minutes and carefully note down the temperature. You will need a thermometer that measures to at least 32°F (0°C).

3
Take out the thermometer and add four or five tablespoon of salt over the ice. Stir it a little.

THINK LIKE A SCIENTIST

What happens when you add salt to frost or snow? Why does the temperature at which it melts drop? Both snow and ice are nothing more than water that has been chilled until it is below 32°F (0°C), assuming a solid form. Covering and then stirring in salt means that it dissolves into the liquid water that covers the pieces of ice. The properties of the water change, and it becomes a saltwater dissolution, like seawater. As you will have found out when you accidentally tasted seawater while on the beach, it can be pretty unpleasant! But it isn't just the flavor that changes; the temperature at which it becomes ice also changes. It isn't 32°F (0°C) anymore, but something even less. As you increase the proportion of salt to water, the temperature required to freeze it continues to drop—you're going to need a new thermometer!

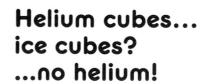

Continue investigating

Add salt to other glasses filled with water, repeating your experiment with different quantities of salt until all of the ice has melted. You can try and refreeze the solution at home, but if you add sufficient salt, it will be impossible to freeze again!

Salt, ice, salt!

A type of dark-colored salt is used on roads in cold places where snow is common, preventing the snow from freezing into ice. While you can still see the snow or ice on the road, it can cause accidents, as cars can skid on the slippery surface.

4

Put the thermometer back and wait a few minutes. Note the temperature and observe what has happened to your ice.

Helium cubes… ice cubes? …no helium!

Helium is the chemical element with the lowest freezing point (the temperature at which it freezes) in the world. Helium is the gas that we use to inflate balloons so that they float in the air! To produce a helium "cube" you would have to chill it to 458°F (236°C)… but there's nowhere that cold in the whole universe!

Hidden treasure

Have you ever wondered what it's like to discover a hoard of buried treasure? Use this experiment to play a cool joke when you go for a day trip—unearth buried treasure! Look around for an empty tin at home—the older the better—and fill it with coins from the age of pirates. Do you want to know how to get them?

What will you need?

- An old tin, preferably metal
- Coins of different sizes
- Paper towel
- Vinegar
- A plate
- Water

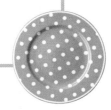

Experiment

Would you like to make coins appear to be hundreds of years old?

1
Find a selection of copper coins of different sizes; 1, 2, and 5 cent coins, for example.

2
Wet the center of a piece of paper towel with a little vinegar, little by little, so that it spreads out slowly.

3
Put the paper towel onto the plate and place the coins on top, leaving space between them.

THINK LIKE A SCIENTIST

Why did the coins age so fast?

Many metals rust as they come in contact with the air.

Over the years they lose their brightness and are eventually covered with a layer of green rust. If you treat 1, 2, and 5 cent coins, it is the copper in them that rusts. This copper reacts with humidity in the air, producing that green coat: copper carbonate. When copper comes into contact with the acetic acid in vinegar, this effect is accelerated. Copper carbonate is produced in just a matter of hours!

Continue investigating

You can reverse this experiment and clean up old coins. Dissolve 10 tablespoons of salt in a glass of vinegar and place the coins inside. One or two days later the coins will be as good as new! Since air cannot reach the coins, the vinegar reacts with the rust and cleans them. The salt speeds this reaction up.

Becker, the money forger

In the nineteenth century, a master counterfeiter named Carl Wihelm Becker made his living producing forged coins in much the same way that you have done in this experiment. There are some coin collectors that still mistake his clever copies for the real thing!

4 Wait for four hours and then take a look at the coins. Now they resemble old coins covered in green rust.

5 Place these aged coins in a tin and take it with you on your next day trip. And always remember to wash your hands after you have handled them!

6 Get your friends to help you bury the tin in a secluded spot, and return to the same spot later with other friends to dig it back up. They will all think that you have found buried treasure!

Raining spores

We propose an experiment in which you will learn more about fungi spores in general and mushrooms in particular.
Did you know that you can classify mushrooms depending on the pattern their spores make as they fall on the floor? There's a technique that permits us to do just this... would you like to try it?

What will you need?

- Different species of fresh mushrooms
- Index cards and pencil

Experiment

Would you like to learn how to make a spore print?

1

Number each of your index cards, and assign each species of mushroom you have collected a number to avoid confusion later on.

2

Pull the stem off the mushroom and place the cap in its natural growing position with its gills pointing downward.

3

Leave the mushroom overnight and carefully lift it the next morning. Look at the pattern that the spores have made. Be careful to avoid wind and drafts that can easily blow the spores away.

THINK LIKE A SCIENTIST

How can this technique be used to classify fungi? How would the spores be dispersed? And what purpose do they serve?

The spore print is the impression that spores form collectively as they fall from the underside of a mature mushroom. The spore print helps us to identify the mushroom, as its color varies across different species. In fact, many fungi are traditionally grouped according to their spore print, whereas in reality we now use new, more sophisticated and trustworthy techniques.

Fungi are immobile organisms that rely on external agents to spread their spores, most commonly the wind. Fungi such as truffles, which grow underground, need a different kind of help, such as boars who dig them up to eat, permitting their spores to be dispersed. Other species give off a smell like putrid meat to attract flies, which act as other dispersing agents.

Spores are a means of reproduction and are also found in mosses and ferns as well as fungi.

Continue investigating

The world of fungi is one of an enormous variety of species, some useful and others lethal. Maybe you would like to find out about poisonous species such as the death cap (*Amanita phalloides*) or the sought-after gastronomic delicacy of truffles (*Tuber sp.*). You can also research species that produce antibiotics (such as penicillin) or those used by other sectors of the food industry (such as yeasts). Finally, you could look into their role in the decomposition of organic matter.

4

Comparing the color of the spores is a useful technique to classify different types of mushrooms!

Can mushrooms be farmed?

Every mushroom produces between 7 and 8 million spores, and although it has not been easy, humans have learned to cultivate a few species of mushrooms. It is very difficult to simulate the mechanism in which mushrooms reproduce and form themselves. Most mushrooms need to establish a very close relationship with other plants, known as mycorrhiza. Mycorrhizal relationships are symbiotic, meaning that the mushroom and plant help each other out and that both of them benefit in some way.

Today, thanks to scientific advances, we can cultivate some species of edible mushroom such as the champignon, oyster mushroom, shiitake, or the highly regarded truffle.

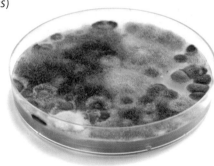

Soils with rhythm

Where does all the rainwater go? It can flow into streams and rivers or drains, form puddles, or be absorbed into the soil. Although rocks, sand, and soil are solid, there are spaces called pores between grains through which water can flow. This porosity varies depending on the type of rock or soil, so the water seeps into the ground at different rates depending on the material.

What will you need?

- A tin of 1.5 liters or more, without lid or base (from canned food, paint, varnish, etc.)
- A hammer
- A plank of wood
- A ruler or tape measure
- A bucket, flask, or bottle that can hold 2 liters of water
- A watch
- 4 inches (10 cm) of masking or duct tape
- Pencil and paper to write down your observations and results
- Water

Experiment

Would you like to know how to test the permeability of soil?

1 Place the tin on the ground with the wooden plank on top. Hit the plank with the hammer until 2 inches (5 cm) of the tin has entered the ground.

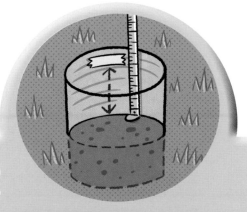

2 Stick your masking or duct tape near the top on the tin, parallel with the top edge. Next, use your ruler to measure the distance from the bottom of the tape to the soil and write it down.

3 Fill the tin with water until it reaches the bottom edge of the tape. Make a note of the time. As the water soaks into the soil, the water level will drop.

THINK LIKE A SCIENTIST

Why do you think that water soaks into some types of terrain more easily than others? Soils with larger grains contain more gaps and water can quickly pass through it, while water percolates more slowly into densely packed soils. Has the speed at which your soil absorbed water remained constant? You will have noticed how it is initially absorbed more rapidly, but as the soil becomes saturated, it becomes unable to hold more water, which remains trapped on the surface.

Very useful clay

Muddy and claylike soils have been used since antiquity to produce tools, utensils, and figurines. The earliest recovered objects date back to the Upper Paleolithic period and represent maternal deities and fertility cults such as the so-called Venus of Dolní Věstonice figurine, which dates from between 29,000–25,000 B.C.

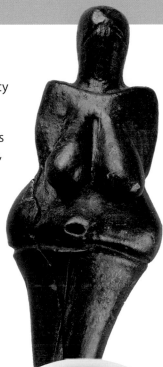

Soil in the movies

Soils are also stars of the silver screen, most famously as quicksand. Quicksand is in fact not sand at all, but rather a mixture of silts completely saturated with water. It is physically impossible for a person to be completely engulfed in quicksand. The real danger is that the victim is trapped and can die of starvation, heat, or exhaustion or not escape nearby floodwaters.

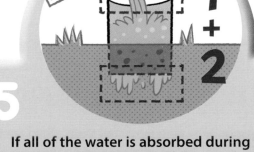

4 Calculate how many inches of water have penetrated the soil by measuring with a ruler the distance between the height of the bottom edge of the tape and the surface of the water at 30 and 60 minutes after pouring the water into the tin. Write these measurements down.

5 If all of the water is absorbed during the course of this experiment, fill the tin back up to your tape marker as before. Any measurements you make from this point on should be noted as the total distance from the soil to the tape, rather than the distance from the water level to the tape.

6 Divide the amount of water absorbed in one hour by 60 to calculate the permeability in inches per minute. Then divide the amount of water absorbed at 30 minutes by 30 to calculate the half-hour permeability inches per minute. Does the water permeate at the same speed for the full hour?

A bat's-eye view

Have you ever been inside a dark cave? Look up at the ceiling; it's covered in bats! Maybe you already know this curious fact about these animals: they may fly like birds, but they are in fact mammals like you and me. Baby bats drink their mother's milk. But there's something even more peculiar... have you ever seen them fly? You would never think they are blind! They travel at great speeds and see not with their eyes but with their ears, calculating the distance to walls and other objects with a type of radar, thanks to echoes.

What will you need?

- A nearby mountain that produces echoes
- A stopwatch
- A friend

Experiment

Would you like to find out how bats see? You will calculate the distance to a wall using only an echo of the sound, just like them.

1
When you go on an outdoor trip, look for a place with a good echo. A good place to try is one with a tall mountain and hardly any nearby trees, so that sound can bounce off and return to you.

2
Clap once and listen carefully to its echo. Say "one" when you clap and "two" when you hear the sound echoed back at you. Practice until you can say "two" a moment before you hear the echo.

3
Now clap and say "two" just before you hear the echo. After this second clap you will hear another echo. Clap a third time, say "three," and clap again.

THINK LIKE A SCIENTIST

How is it possible to calculate the distance to the mountain counting claps?

When you clap, your hands beat the air very quickly and create a wave of sound, similar to the wave created on the surface of water when you throw a stone. Sound waves always travel through the air at the same speed (1/4 mile per second). If you could calculate how many seconds pass before you hear the echo of your clap, you could figure out how far away the mountain is. You would have to multiply the seconds you count by 340 and then divide the result by 2, because the sound wave has traveled in both directions during this time.

Well, with this experiment you have succeeded! Let's imagine that you clapped 120 times in 60 seconds (one minute). If you divide those 60 seconds by your 120 claps, you will see that 0.5 seconds is the time between each clap, or between a clap and its echo. If you now multiply this time by 340, you will figure out how far the sound has traveled in both directions to and from the mountain.

Notice that the formula you have used to calculate the distance is 60 multiplied by 340 and then divided by 2 (10,200), with this number divided by the number of claps.

Bats and radar

This experiment has taught you how radar works. Radar is a device that detects objects via sound waves. It omits a sound and then calculates the distance just like you did, depending on how long it takes to receive an echo. This means that it can be used to detect faraway airplanes, submarines under the sea, or clouds loaded with rainwater. But what is most surprising is that this is exactly how bats see! Their brains create images of the objects around them by calculating the time it takes for sound to travel and return to them.

Continue investigating

If you are on a trip to the countryside and hear distant thunder, you can use the same principle to calculate how far you are from the storm.

Notice how flashes of light in the sky—lightning—always occur before thunderclaps. Because light travels much faster than sound (it can travel six times around the world in 1 second!), you see the lightning in the same moment that it occurs. Count how many seconds before you hear thunder and multiply by 340. This figure will tell you how far away the storm is in meters.

4 Continue to count off echoes as "one," "two," "three," "four" until these numbers coincide with the echoes of your claps. Practice a bit until you build up a consistent rhythm and your claps coincide with each echo.

5 Ask a friend to count how many times you clap in a minute on the stopwatch.

6 Divide 10,200 by the number of claps in a minute. This is the distance in meters to your mountain!

Salty stalactites

Have you ever been to visit a cave full of stalactites and stalagmites? Do you know that they take thousands of years to form? Draw yourself a picture to remind yourself what they look like, because with this simple experiment you are going to create your own stalactites and stalagmites in just one week!

What will you need?

- A small plate
- Two glasses
- Water
- Salt
- Cotton thread
- Paper clips
- Tablespoon
- A spoon
- Scissors

Experiment

Are you ready to make salt stalactites?

1
Half-fill two glasses with hot water. You can heat them in a microwave, but for no more than one minute.

2
Add 6 tablespoons of salt to each glass and stir them thoroughly so that the only remaining salt is the salt on the bottom of the glass that will not dissolve.

3
Add hot water to each glass and stir the water until the salt has dissolved completely.

THINK LIKE A SCIENTIST

How did the stalactites form?

If you closely examine the kitchen salt through a magnifying glass, you will see that it consists of small crystals. When the water in both glasses evaporates after a few days, the salt returns to its solid state and also crystallizes. But this does not only occur inside glasses or other containers; the saltwater soaks upwards through the cotton thread until it reaches the point between the glasses. From here, it drips slowly onto the plate, and every drop that evaporates creates a small salt crystal, little by little, forming a stalactite. Since the drops of water do not remain intact as they fall, sometimes it can be difficult for a stalagmite to form… but the hanging thread will make it easier for the water to hold on to salt crystals, gradually forming a larger and larger vertical column… the stalactite.

Compare the results to the picture that you drew before!

Continue investigating

Other materials (such as aspirin) can also produce spectacular crystal effects as they evaporate. Add 10 aspirin to a glass jar full of water, cover with a cloth, and wait until the water evaporates. Be patient because this could take months… but the crystals that form are incredible and the result is spectacular!

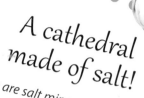

A cathedral made of salt!

There are salt mines all over the world. These are mined for their sea salt that has crystallized over millions of years and can now be taken away and used to make table salt that you can put into your salt shaker. But some of these salt mines are very special. In the Wieliczka mine, near the city of Krakow in Poland, miners have created beautiful sculptures and even dug out an entire cathedral! In the Zipaquira salt mine near Bogota in Colombia, there is a spectacular underground salt cathedral.

4 Cut yourself a piece of cotton thread about a handspan in length and attach a paper clip to each end.

5 Place one end into each glass of water so that the clips sink to the bottom, leaving a length of thread suspended between the glasses and over the small plate.

6 Wait for a week until all of the water has evaporated (the water will evaporate more quickly in the summer). You will see that a stalactite has formed and is hanging from the wire, while with a bit of luck you will have a stalagmite on the plate!

The color race

Most leaves and flowers are a particular color, but that changes when they die. Have you ever thought why this happens? Were the new colors already there, or have some colors appeared and others disappeared? You can investigate this yourself!

What will you need?

- Dark green leaves that you find in the countryside
- A couple spoonfuls of clean sand (you can use beach sand if you wash it several times to get rid of any clay)
- A mortar and pestle
- A dropper
- Household solvent, such as acetone
- A strip of clean, absorbent paper (coffee-filter type)
- A strainer
- A spoon
- A glass

Experiment

Would you like to learn how to separate different pigments found in leaves and flowers?

1 Take a sample of green leaves. Place them in the mortar with a little sand and one or two drops of solvent (acetone).

2 Crush the sample with the pestle and strain the resulting extract through a fine sieve into a glass. The extract must be well concentrated.

3 Take a coffee filter and cut a rectangle strip that is 1.5 inches (4 cm) wide, 0.75 inches (2 cm) higher than the top of your glass. Use the dropper to place a drop of acetone about 1 inch (3 cm) from the base, and leave it to stand for a few minutes until the excess solvent has evaporated.

THINK LIKE A SCIENTIST

What are the different stripes of colors that appear in the filter paper?

Why do they appear separately?

If the leaves were green, why do they produce yellow and orange pigments?

The orange, yellow, and green colored stripes correspond to the primary pigments that are found in leaves (carotenes, xanthophylls, and chlorophylls).

The pigments appear separately because they move at different speeds.

Yellow and orange pigments are present in leaves, but they are masked by chlorophylls. When the leaves die chlorophylls quickly disappear, but the other pigments stay for a much longer time.

Continue investigating

You can follow the same procedure to separate the different pigments that flowers use to display their bright colors. Use a variety of wildflowers of different colors.

You can also mix different colored inks and later separate them using chromatography.

4

Add a little acetone to the glass—no more than 0.75 inches (2 cm) deep. Place your strip of filter paper into the glass so that the pigment that you have added with the dropper does not touch the solvent. Wait until the solvent soaks up the filter paper, reaching the top.

The unbeatable detective

In the United States in 1989, a mother was convicted of poisoning her baby with antifreeze. However, a second investigation, conducted with a type of precision chromatography, revealed that the substance that caused the death of her child was not antifreeze but a molecule produced as a result of a rare genetic mutation. Thanks to chromatography, the mother was cleared of murder and immediately released.

Chromatography

This is a technique that allows scientists to separate "delicate" substances without altering them. There are different types of chromatography: using fine paper (that you have used in this experiment), liquid, or gas, although these last two techniques require complicated and expensive equipment.

Chromatography is not only useful for scientists, but it has also become one of the most useful tools for investigating criminal activity.

Frothy soils

The organic material present in soil is a result of the decomposition of creatures that live above it and biological activity of the creatures that live within it (such as worms, insects of all kinds, microorganisms, etc.). When these remains and metabolic waste are broken down, they become something that is called humus.

What will you need?

- A garden trowel (to dig up your soil samples)
- 2 different soil samples (one containing a lot of humus and another containing very little)
- A plastic or glass beaker
- Hydrogen peroxide
- Notebook and pen

Experiment

Would you like to learn how to check if there is organic material in soil?

None: No bubbles are produced (contains no organic matter).
Light: A few bubbles are produced (organic matter is present in small quantities).
Strong: A lot of bubbles are produced (organic matter is present in large quantities).

1

Before you carry out this experiment, closely examine your soil samples. Pay close attention to the presence of roots and other larger pieces of organic material such as leaves, snails, worms, or other bugs… be sure to remove all of them before you continue.

2

Put your samples into a beaker and add some hydrogen peroxide. If it begins to bubble, this indicates the presence of organic material. Be careful with soils with a very high content of organic material; it is best to add the hydrogen peroxide little by little, because the reaction can be quite dramatic!

3

Draw up a table in your notebook as we have suggested here, and use it to record your results. Is there a difference in color between soils that contain a large amount of organic material and those that contain little?

THINK LIKE A SCIENTIST

Why does the organic material present in the soil bubble when it comes into contact with the hydrogen peroxide?

Hydrogen peroxide (H_2O_2) is used to demonstrate the presence of organic material in soil because the organic matter decomposes in normal water and releases oxygen as it reacts. The more gas is produced, the more organic material the soil contains.

Continue investigating

You can use a procedure similar to the one explained here to determine the calcium carbonate content of the soil. You will need an adult to prepare a 20% solution of hydrochloric acid (*aqua fortis*). Add a few drops of acid to the soil sample, and if bubbles form they indicate the presence of carbonates. The more bubbles there are the greater the carbonate content of the soil.

Soil that burns

Large amounts of partially decomposed organic matter (mainly grasses and leaves) accumulate in peat bogs due to cold, damp climates and low levels of oxygen. We are able to exploit the high carbon content in these marshy and generally unproductive areas by extracting fuel for fires that replaces wood.

Food for soils

The presence of organic material in soils is essential for its fertility and cultivability. Soils without organic materials are poor soils whose physical properties cannot support plant growth. Intensive cultivation can result in rapid consumption of nutrient chemicals, which need to be replaced through the application of chemical fertilizers or organic fertilizers such as manure, guano, potash, or compost.

1 2 3

GARDEN FLOWERPOT BEACH

4

You can carry out this experiment with different types of soil, recording results in your table as you go.

Predict what the weather will be like tomorrow

You've been exploring the outdoors with friends for a few days. There's no TV, cell phone service, or radio... but you want to know what the weather will be like the following day. We suggest that you make a simple barometer that will measure atmospheric pressure and tell you if it will rain or be sunny.

What will you need?

- A balloon
- A glass jar
- A straw
- A shoe box
- A rubber band
- Scissors
- Glue
- A pencil

Experiment

Would you like you know what the weather will be like tomorrow? Become an expert meteorologist with this simple experiment.

1 Be sure to choose a sunny day to begin this experiment so you will be able to better understand how to read your barometer.

2 Cut your balloon and completely cover the top of the jar with it, as if you were making a drum. Pull it tight so that you have to push a little with your finger to make a depression, then fix it in place with the rubber band.

3 Affix one end of the straw to the center of the balloon so that it protrudes horizontally.

THINK LIKE A SCIENTIST

Why did the straw on your barometer move?

The air above your head weighs something. This weighs down on your head and your whole body, but you don't notice it because you are so used to it being there. For example, if you are traveling by car and you quickly open the window, air pressure will suddenly drop. You will experience a strange sensation in your ears as the air "pushes" its way in from outside.

When you seal your jar with the balloon, the interior and exterior air pressure remains the same across the surface of the balloon and it remains flat. The air pressure outside of the jar, called atmospheric pressure, might have changed the following day, although the pressure inside the jar remains the same. If the atmospheric pressure drops, the air inside the jar pushes the balloon up and the end of the straw drops. If the atmospheric pressure rises, the air outside of the jar pushes the balloon downward and the end of the straw rises.

If there is high atmospheric pressure it is called an anticyclone; the sky is free of clouds and humidity and good weather are on its way. If the atmospheric pressure is low, there might be a storm… don't forget your umbrella!

A map of the weather

If you look at a weather chart you will see how meteorologists use atmospheric pressure to predict weather. They collect data from barometers all around the world and connect points that have equal atmospheric pressure with lines. These are the circles that are marked with an H (for high atmospheric pressure) or an L (low atmospheric pressure). By doing this, they can predict what the weather will be like the next day anywhere in the world!

Continue investigating

As you climb a mountain, the amount of air surrounding you gradually decreases. Some mountains are so tall that you would struggle to breathe at the top! You can use your barometer to measure the change in air pressure by noting the position of the straw before you start to climb and again when you reach the peak.

4

Stick the jar at the bottom of the shoe box so that the straw almost touches the side.

5

Draw a horizontal line on the inside wall of the box, at the same height as the straw.

6

Have a look at the straw the next day. If it has not moved or has risen above the line, there is an anticyclone, meaning good weather! However, if it has dropped below the line, a storm may be on its way… it might rain!

Chameleonic flowers

P lants do not have a "heart" to pump their sap. Have you ever wondered how water reaches their leaves from their roots?

You'll find out how and will also learn to magically change the color of your flowers in the experiment.

Experiment

What will you need?

- A white flower with its stem and leaves, about 8 inches (20 cm) in total length (like a white carnation)
- A small pair of scissors
- Two small, narrow glasses
- Red and blue paint mixed with water

Would you like to see how sap conquers gravity and travels up the tallest capillaries in a plant?

1

One day when you're outside pick a white flower with large petals and a long, thick stem. Cut the stem so that it extends about 8 inches (20 cm) below the flower.

2

↕ 2 in.

Use your scissors to separate the stem into two halves lengthwise about 2 inches (5 cm) below the flower.

3

Put two small glasses next to each other. Put watered-down red paint in one and watered-down blue paint in the other.

THINK LIKE A SCIENTIST

How does the paint reach the flower petals?

Which characteristics should your glasses have so that the sap can rise?

The sap, and in the case of this experiment paint, rises from the glasses through the plant's capillaries. Trees feed through their roots, with some taking sap more than 490 feet (150 m) above the ground. These capillaries must be incredibly thin (70 or 80 thousandths of a millimeter), and the leaves have to evaporate (or sweat out) some of the water that rises, causing lower pressure inside the glass.

Continue investigating

If you don't have a white flower, you can also use a lettuce leaf. Choose one of the interior leaves that is almost white because it has not been exposed to light.

Separate the petiole and submerge each half in a different glass. If you use food coloring instead of paint, you can still eat the lettuce after!

Florist painters

Some florists use this mechanism to surprise us with dazzling ornamental flowers whose colors do not exist in the natural world. However, making colors more beautiful than those in nature is surely an impossible task.

4

Submerge the two halves of the stem in different glasses and wait a few hours. Your flower will be multicolored, as if it were a chameleon.

The myth of the black rose

There are many different colored roses, but no black ones. However, some clever con artists have attempted to sell roses they claim are naturally black, when in fact they have been colored artificially. The closest to a natural black rose are two varieties of intensely red-colored roses known as the black baccarat and black pearl.

Soil made to order

Not all soils are created the same way. Each can be classified, and it is worth knowing the differences (composition, porosity, grain size, acidity, organic content). If you know this, you can easily tell which kind of soil you have. In this experiment you will be able to observe different sizes and densities of the components that make up soils.

Experiment

What will you need?

- Plastic bags
- Clear glass jars with lids (their size may vary depending on how much sample material you wish to analyze)
- Earth samples from different sediment layers or very different soils
- Water
- Pencil
- Notebook

In just a few steps you can see the different components in soil. All you need is water and soil!

1 Take soil samples from different sites and store them separately in your plastic bags. Note where you have taken the samples from on each bag.

2 Fill the first jar about ¾ full with soil from one of the bags. Write down the place of the soil's origin. Next, add water until the jar is full.

3 Tightly close the jar with the lid and shake it vigorously. Leave it to rest for a few hours until the soil has settled.

THINK LIKE A SCIENTIST

The soil sits in the jars and forms bands or layers depending on the content of each sample. Heavier particles (gravel and sand) settle first, forming a paler-colored layer, while lighter sediments (silts and clays) settle above, forming darker-colored layers. Organic matter will be floating on top of the jar.

Beware of the clays!

Impermeable terrain consists of clay, silt, marl, and gypsum, which form soils that expand, or increase in volume, when they absorb water. In contrast, when they dry out, their volume decreases and they crack in a curious, mosaic-like way. This can cause serious construction problems (buildings cracking, loss of stability in foundations and walls...) and misshapen pavements and roads.

Continue investigating

A more technical method to separate different soil components according to size is by using a sieve. Sieving is a practical method to separate a mishmash of components. It involves passing a mixture of particles of different sizes through a strainer or sieve. The smaller particles will drop through the holes, while the larger particles are retained inside the strainer or sieve. For example, if you pick up soils and dust it through the sieve, the smaller soil particles will pass through the holes, while larger particles such as pebbles will be retained in the sieve.

GRANULOMETRIC GRADING

PARTICLE	SCALE
Clays	<0,002 mm
Limes	0,002-0,06 mm
Sands	0,06-2 mm
Gravels	2-60 mm
Round pebbles	60-250 mm
Stones	>250 mm

4 Follow the same process for each of your soil samples. Are they all the same? Where is the organic material (humus, roots, leaves, etc.) that was in the soil?

5 Draw a picture of each of the sediment deposits in the jar and compare results between each of your samples.

A name for every grain of earth

Normally the name "soil" is applied to all of its components, but scientists classify each "soil" differently, depending on size. The size of some grains of soil can be estimated at a glance, but for some smaller grains it may require a magnifying glass. This table will help you to classify each grain.

Making a rainbow disappear

W ish for a little rain on your next trip outside, because with a little luck, when it stops and the sun comes up, you will see a fabulous rainbow! This magical natural phenomenon combines colors in an arc of light. But you're even more magical... because you're going to make it disappear!

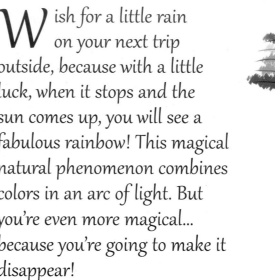

Experiment

Would you like to see a rainbow disappear before your very eyes?

What will you need?

- A hose with sprinkler or spray attachment
- 3D glasses (try the glasses that are sold in movie theaters to watch films in three dimensions)
- A friend

1 If you don't see natural rainbows, you can use a hose with a sprinkler or spray attachment. Position yourself with your back to the sun.

2 Get a friend to spray the water in front of you. Of course, you can do this yourself, but you will need both hands for the experiment. That is why it is better to ask for help.

3 Take note! The rainbow will appear in the same direction as your shadow! If it is near dawn or dusk—that is, if the sun is lower in the sky—your shadow will be longer and the rainbow will be larger and even more impressive.

THINK LIKE A SCIENTIST

Why can we sometimes see a rainbow? And how is it possible to make it disappear?

White light from the sun is a composite of all colors of the rainbow. When the sun's rays pass through drops of water in the air, each color travels in a different direction and we can see them separately. The effect that these rays produce as they travel in different directions forms a rainbow.

If it were possible to examine its light closely with a very strong magnifying glass, we would see that it is made of tiny "balls" of energy, called photons. The photons in a rainbow have their own very special characteristic: they are not ball-shaped but are flat, like tiny coins, and all of them are oriented in the same direction. Scientists say that they are "polarized." Well, 3D glasses from the movie theater have a kind of grid that only allows the photons to pass in one way, as coins will only fit in your piggy bank if their orientation is matched with the slot. They are polarized glasses. If they are turned at an angle, the photons of the rainbow cannot pass through their grid and will not reach your eyes… and the rainbow disappears!

Continue investigating

Find yourself a pair of 3D glasses, put them on, and squint through one eye. Can you see anything? Have a good look! One of the two lenses appears totally black. And if the other eye squints, then the other lens will seem dark. Can you guess why? The right lens does not allow light from the left lens to pass because their "grids" are crossed.

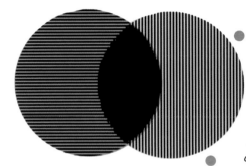

Using polarized light to find the way home

Polarized light occurs not only in a rainbow but also in the light of a blue sky. Some creatures, such as tarantulas and bees, use the way that polarized light is oriented to find their homes or their next meal!

4

Pick up your 3D glasses and look through one lens while you cover the other eye with your hand. Gradually tilt the lens and see how the rainbow slowly disappears!

3D movies

3D cinemas project two separate images onto the screen at once—one that you view with your right eye and the other that you view with your left eye. The light from each image contains polarized photons, such as those found in a rainbow. However, one of the images is oriented to "cross" the other. The "grids" in each lens of the polarized glasses align the two images, one perpendicular to the other, so they can separate the image that corresponds to each eye. Your brain sees a distinct image through each eye and believes that it's seeing things as they are in reality—in three dimensions!

Midnight feast

Maybe you've found balls or cylinders of hair while walking outside. Scientists call these pellets, and they are not to be confused with excrement. Pellets are a regurgitated (or vomited) mass of hair and bone naturally produced by nocturnal birds that are unable to digest them.

Would you like to become a forensic detective who is able to analyze and find out what these extraordinary birds feed on?

Experiment

What will you need?

- Pellets
- Fine tweezers
- A jug of water (optional)
- A guidebook to birds and mammals

Carefully separate the bones inside the pellets and discover the favorite delicacies of nocturnal birds of prey.

1 Find one or several pellets outside. They are often found at the base of trees or around abandoned or isolated buildings.

2 Use your tweezers to carefully separate the bones. If this proves difficult, you can dip them in lukewarm water first.

3 Pay special attention to skulls and jawbones, the most useful for identifying their original owners.

THINK LIKE A SCIENTIST

What advantage is there in studying pellets?

Why do the bones remain whole?

Studying pellets is an easy way to find out which species of rodents and birds of prey live in a given area. Consider that otherwise observing nocturnal animals would be uncomfortable and complicated.

Nocturnal birds of prey have a night vision that is much more developed than our own. In addition, their flight is virtually silent and imperceptible to human ears.

The bones remain whole because birds of prey swallow their food whole rather than chew it, digesting the soft parts and discarding the rest through their mouths.

Continue investigating

Common owls, barn owls, tawny owls, and little owls are extraordinary predators, but not only for their night vision and silent flight. They play an important part in maintaining ecosystems by controlling the number of rodents, which can breed very quickly. For this reason, many countries protect these birds by law.

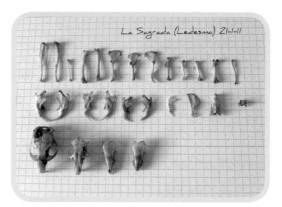

La Sagrada (Ledesma) 21-1-11

Investigate how these birds have adapted to their nocturnal existence, paying close attention to the size of their eyes and the extraordinary flexibility of their necks.

Some people believe that nocturnal predators can turn their heads around totally (that is, 360°), but this is not true. They can certainly turn their heads to both the left and the right much further than other animals, and more quickly, but they are really a long way from being "exorcist" birds.

Myths and superstitions

For some cultures, meeting a nocturnal predator is bad luck; because of their nocturnal habits, they are considered harbingers of death.

4

Use your guidebook to try and find out which bird of prey has produced the pellet, based on the rodents that they have consumed.

However, in classical Greece, the barn owl was symbolic of Athena, goddess of wisdom and protector of the city of Athens. That is why barn owls appear on euros that have been minted in Greece.

ΕΛΛΑΣ ΔΡ. 3.50

The collapsing castle

At one time you may have seen a news article about landslides that have blocked roads or even buried entire villages. This is a natural process and is reliant on many factors, including the composition of terrain. In this experiment you will build a sand castle and learn how important this is.

Experiment

What will you need?

- Two beach pails and a sand shovel
- Distilled water
- Tap water
- Seawater (if you live near to the sea)
- A washing bowl
- Salt
- Sand
- A pitcher
- A spoon
- A plastic tray or other flat surface that can serve as a base for your castles

In this experiment you can observe how important the substances that bind soils together are.

1

Fill the pitcher with seawater. If you are not near to the sea, use tap water, adding a good quantity of salt.

2

Fill the washing bowl with beach sand. If you are not near the sea, use the most similar sand you can find. Try the sandpit in your local park, a garden, or building site near your house.

3

Fill your beach pail with sand, adding saltwater until the sand sticks together, and make a sand castle on a flat surface (for example, a plastic tray). Try not to add too much water to the sand because it will become unstable and collapse as soon as it comes out of the bucket.

THINK LIKE A SCIENTIST

Which of the two castles is more robust?

Some materials get their strength from cements, which bind grains together, meaning that the castle made with saltwater is stronger than the castles made with distilled and tap water. In nature, soils containing calcium carbonate cement are more unstable than those with silica cement because acid rainwater dissolves the carbonated cement more easily.

Continue investigating

Investigate how water can help to maintain cohesive fine material in soils (fine sand, clay, and silt). Investigate how too much water can cause the soil to flow in a similar way to liquid. Place dry, fine soil into an inclined length of guttering and slowly add more and more water. You will see that initially, the water prevents the soil from flowing, but when there is an excessive amount of water, the soil flows like a river of mud.

A peculiar word: "lahar"

A lahar is a type of mud flow caused by the rapid melting of snow or glaciers during a volcanic eruption. They cause a rapid increase in water content within soils and flow just like a river. Lahars can be extremely dangerous because they move at high speed over several miles, causing catastrophic destruction along the way.

4 Make another sand castle right next to the first, but this time use distilled water to give consistency to the sand. If you do not have any distilled water, use tap water.

5 Leave the sand castles in the sun to dry. After a while one castle will collapse before the other.

Blocked roads

It is not uncommon to hear news about roads blocked by landslides and rockfalls during local rainy seasons. These problems are typically caused by a decrease in the consistency of the soil, combined with a high clay content, which means that the soil absorbs large quantities of water. On other occasions, landslides are caused by sloping roadsides that have been cut to an excessive angle.

Magical wine glasses

After spending the morning splashing water and making sand castles, it's time for a meal! Would you like to entertain dinner guests with an experiment that will leave them speechless?

What will you need?

- Two wine glasses
- A slightly rigid piece of paper (not a paper napkin)
- A little sand
- Water

Experiment

Did you know that it is possible to draw with sound?

1 Choose a pair of wine glasses and position them closely together.

2 Cover one of the wine glasses with a piece of paper, and sprinkle a little sand on top of the paper.

3 Wet your finger with a little water and gently run it around the entire rim of the wine glass continually, until the glass produces a sound similar to a flute.

THINK LIKE A SCIENTIST

Why do pictures form on the other glass without you touching it?

This experiment allows us to observe the phenomenon of resonance. Remember that sound is vibration of the air. By making noise with the first wine glass, the air around it vibrates. These vibrations reach the second glass, pushing it backward and forward and making it produce noise, albeit softly. You can check this by repeating the experiment without paper or sand. Sound the first glass and quickly place your hand on it to stop it from vibrating; the other glass will be making an audible noise due to resonance.

When you place the paper over the second glass, these vibrations are spread across the paper, moving the grains of sand. Exactly the same thing happens when you sit on the middle of a trampoline while someone else is jumping on it. The grains of sand make for some very peculiar pictures!

Gateshead Millennium Bridge

Continue investigating

Try filling the cup that you are sounding with water to different levels. You will hear that the note, or sound it produces, will differ according to the amount of water inside... and the picture that it will make over the other glass will also be different.

The Millennium Bridge

A similar phenomenon to that which moved the grains of sand caused London's Millennium Bridge to close on the day of its inauguration in the year 2000. The vibrations caused by the footsteps of more than 90,000 people who crossed it resulted in resonance, and the bridge started to vibrate more than necessary. Engineers had to close it down and fix it. It was reopened at a later date.

4

Now look at the sand on top of the paper. It's magically forming itself into pictures without anyone touching the other wine glass!

Musical instrument tuners

Musicians use resonators similar to that which you created with two wine glasses to accurately tune musical instruments. The apparatus is manufactured to "hear" an assigned musical note, indicating when it is played. When the musician plays an instrument and the apparatus doesn't resonate "properly," it is shown on a screen so that the musician can then tune it correctly.

Danger: Corrosive beach!

How beautiful beaches can be! Many of them belong on a postcard. But the inhabitants know that living close to the beach can have its problems. Take a look at the balcony railings and door hinges. Some of them are rusty! Do you know why? Find out with this experiment!

What will you need?

- Three glasses
- Tap water
- Seawater (if you are not close to the sea, you can add salt to river or lake water)
- Three long screws
- Pencil and notebook

Experiment

Would you like to find out why iron near the beach spoils?

1

Pour a little water into two glasses, one seawater and the other tap water, and leave the third glass empty. Use transparent glasses so that you can observe what is happening inside them.

2

Put one screw in each glass so that half of each screw remains out of the water, and leave them for a whole day. Observe any changes and record them in your notebook.

3

The next day, take out the screws that have been in the glass containing tap water and the empty glass. They will be practically the same as they were when you left them.

THINK LIKE A SCIENTIST

Why did the screw submerged in seawater rust so quickly?

What is the orange-colored substance that has appeared on its surface?

When iron is in contact with the air, a chemical reaction slowly occurs: the oxygen in the air combines with the iron to form a new, orange-colored substance called iron oxide. But this is a slow process and you won't see it happen in only one day. This is why the screws in the empty glass and the glass containing tap water remain as they were before, whereas the screw in seawater has quickly rusted—in only one day! This is because the seawater, which contains salt, accelerates this chemical reaction. This is why iron spoils so quickly, such as on balcony railings and door hinges in homes close to the sea. After a long time the rust can even completely eat through iron!

Continue investigating

Once you have rusted all three screws, you can remove the rust with another chemical reaction. All you have you do is place them in some kind of acid for a few hours. Try soaking the screws in three glasses: one containing lemon juice (citric acid), one containing vinegar (acetic acid), and the third containing a cola drink (phosphoric acid).

Which glass cleans the screws more quickly?

The airplane convertible

In 1988, a Boeing 737 was flying over the Pacific Ocean when suddenly its roof flew off! Luckily all 90 passengers on board had securely fastened their seatbelts. The pilot had to make an emergency landing in Hawaii. Quite scary! This accident was caused by a ceiling cracked by corrosion!

4

Next, remove the screw that was in the glass containing seawater. The screw is covered in an orange color. It has rusted, a process that is called "corrosion."

Oil avoids rusting

Consider that oil is often used to prevent iron from rust. Door hinges, door locks, and bicycle chains are all lubricated with a spray that contains oil. Do you know why? The oil acts as a protective shield: it stops the oxygen from coming into contact with the iron so that it does not react with it and cannot rust!

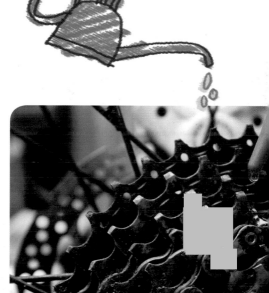

Water cycle in miniature

Water is an extraordinary substance because all life depends on its existence: where there is water, there is life! It is the single element on our planet that can be found in three states in its natural form—solid (ice), liquid (water), and gas (water vapor)—with the ability to continually change between one form and another (the water cycle).

Water is a completely renewable resource (if its quantity remains unchanged), although not everyone has access to clean drinking water.

What will you need?

- Two different sized bowls, one that can fit inside the other
- Enough plastic wrap to cover the larger bowl
- A pot to boil water
- Salt
- A small stone (a coin will also work)
- An adult

Experiment

Would you like to find out how the water cycle works?

1 Put salt into the pot of water. Get a grown-up to help you boil it.

2 While the water is heating up, put the smaller bowl inside the larger bowl.

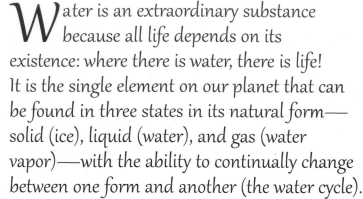

3 When the water starts to boil, ask an adult to help you pour it into the larger bowl.

THINK LIKE A SCIENTIST

Look at the water in the small bowl. How do you think it got there?

Sip the water in the small bowl. Why do you think that it tastes so good?

By heating up the water we have made it evaporate—that is, it transforms from its liquid state to a gaseous state. When this steam touches the plastic film, it cools and condensates (reverts from a gaseous state back to a liquid state), moves down the incline of the plastic wrap and drops into the smaller bowl.

But the salt dissolved in the water has not undergone this process and has stayed in the large bowl. The water in the small bowl is therefore distilled water rather than saltwater.

Continue investigating

What would happen if we add food coloring to the hot water? Would this also end up in the small bowl? Repeat the experiment and give it a try.

A precious resource, only available for the few

Millions of people around the world do not have access to drinking water and must walk many miles to fetch water free from contamination and dangerous microorganisms. Only 3% of the water on Earth is safe to drink, meaning that only relatively few people have access to it.

This problem could be solved if everyone could create a cheap, effective apparatus to distill water, as we have done in this experiment.

Water wars

In the year 2000, the Bolivian government privatized the supply of drinking water in the city of Cochabamba, resulting in a rise in price of more than 50%. This caused outrage among the citizens, and the government was obliged to reverse the decision in order to avoid a massacre. The social, political, and economic consequences of a shortage in drinking water are potent destabilizing factors. The control of water will cause violent conflict in the near future, just as nations now go to war over oil.

4 Quickly cover both bowls with plastic wrap, so it is airtight, sealing the steam inside.

5 Place the stone above the middle of the small bowl. Check first that the stone makes a small depression in the plastic wrap but does not tear it.

6 Wait one or two hours and then see what has happened to the water that has evaporated from the larger bowl.

The Himalayas in 30 seconds

In this activity we will use a device to simulate the tectonic folding that produced the earth's mountain ranges. We can use the device to simulate the forces that are produced in certain parts of the Earth as a result of the collision between two tectonic plates. Constructing this model will help you understand how mountain chains were formed from stratified rock.

Experiment

What will you need? ←

- Small plastic or glass transparent container, such as a fish tank
- A wooden board that fits inside the container
- Dry sand
- Flour or other powder that is in contrast to the color of your sand

The Himalayas were formed when tectonic plates caused India and Asia to collide. Would you like to simulate what happened to the seabed when these two continental masses came together?

1 Place a wooden board against one side of the transparent container.

2 Alternately, overlay multiple layers of dry sand and flour in the transparent container, but no more than half full.

3 Very carefully push the wooden board across the container so that it compresses the layers, pausing from time to time to observe the results.

THINK LIKE A SCIENTIST

Natural forces act to misshape rocks. When you begin to move the wooden board, the force it applies is sufficient to overcome the sand's natural friction, "folding" it. This force also works against gravity, causing the sand to rise. Note how plastic deformation (folding) occurs first and fracturing or faulting (brittle deformation) occurs if you keep applying force to the sand (fragile misshapenness).

Continue investigating

Alternately, repeat the experiment with layers of sand and flour, but use two wooden boards to cause movement on both sides of your container. Push one board more quickly or harder than the other. Do you form the same folds or faults? Try to repeat the experiment with different materials—coarser or finer, more consistent or less consistent, etc. Do these materials behave in the same way as the sand and flour?

Marine fossils in the Himalayas

How is it possible that the rocks that form the Himalayas contain fossils of marine creatures? The explanation is that the rocks that make up these mountains once formed a seabed. When the Indian subcontinent collided with Asia about 55 million years ago, the pressure that was generated between the folds lifted up a huge amount of marine sediments accumulated at the bottom of the sea between the two plates, forming the Himalayas.

What's more, it shakes!

The clash of tectonic plates not only forms mountain ranges but also causes earthquakes and volcanoes. The plates are in contact with each other like huge icebergs. If they crash into each other or separate, they produce earthquakes at their edges. This plate movement is a result of huge fractures in the Earth's crust. Energy is released in the form of mechanical waves, which vibrate their way to the Earth's surface.

Drawing with sand

$x = A\sin(\omega_x t + \alpha)$
$y = B\sin(\omega_y t + \beta)$
$\delta = \alpha - \beta$

Did you know that math, in addition to helping us work out equations in our everyday lives, can also be used to create authentic works of art? Become an accomplished mathematician with this experiment, creating a work of art using the movement of a bottle.

What will you need?

- A plastic bottle
- Long and short pieces of rope
- Sand
- A smooth, picture-free towel
- A tree from which to hang the rope and bottle
- Scissors
- Screwdriver

Experiment

Did you know that it is possible to draw a beautiful picture with sand using just a moving bottle? Here's how it's done!

1

Cut the base from the bottle and make a small hole in the lid.

2

Make two small holes in the plastic, near the bottom of the bottle so that they are opposite to each other across the bottle.

3

Thread the long piece of rope through one of the holes and tie a knot. Pass the short rope through the other hole and tie it to the first, as shown in the picture above.

THINK LIKE A SCIENTIST

Why do these spectacular pictures form on the towel?

The bottle swings back and forth if you push it. If you push it carefully directly away from you, it will draw a straight line on the towel. But if you push it in any other direction, it will swing in a more complicated way. This is a combination of two oscillating movements that will form a beautiful drawing called the Lissajous curve. These figures were discovered two centuries ago by French mathematician and physicist Jules Antoine Lissajous, who explained them using simple mathematical formulas.

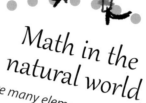

Continue investigating

Try pushing the bottle harder or more gently and in different directions. Each variation will result in the bottle moving in a different way and drawing different pictures on the towel!

Math in the natural world

There are many elements of nature that can be expressed as mathematical formulas, such as Lissajous' figures. Take a close look at a snail shell, how the sections of a pineapple rind fit together, or at the wind eddies that power hurricanes: they are all a kind of spiral! Did you know that even your fingernails would end up in a spiral if you allowed them to grow long enough? Some cauliflowers and fern leaves are formed by fractals, which can also be written with mathematical formulas.

4 Tie the other end of the rope to a tree branch.

5 Place a smooth, picture-free towel underneath the bottle.

6 Fill the bottle with sand and push it gently so that it moves back and forth. Look at the towel… the sand is forming a spectacular picture!

Make them shine!

You probably love to collect seashells, looking for them in the sand along the seashore! They're beautiful! Sometimes they contain the remains of their owners, but how would you like to make them as good as new, or even make fantastic necklaces with them? Would you like to learn a trick to clean them really well?

What will you need?

- A transparent glass
- White vinegar
- Seashells and conch shells
- Soap and water

VINEGAR

Experiment

Do you want to learn how to totally clean seashells and conch shells?

1

Fill a transparent glass with white vinegar and put your shells inside so that the vinegar covers them completely.

2

Examine the surface of the shells. You will see that they are forming and giving off small bubbles that float to the surface of the vinegar.

2-3h

3

Leave the shells inside the water for two or three hours, then remove them.

THINK LIKE A SCIENTIST

Why did the vinegar clean the shells? And why do bubbles form on the surface of the shells?

Seashells and conch shells are skeletons of small marine creatures called mollusks, which have a skeleton inside of their bodies instead of on the outside. The shells are formed over the course of their lives by the calcium carbonate dissolved in seawater. When you put a shell into the glass, the vinegar, which is an acid (acetic acid), reacts with the calcium carbonate, corroding it and forming a gas (carbon dioxide). This gas is exactly what forms the bubbles. The external layers of the shell are removed, making it shine!

Continue investigating

You can leave your shells in the vinegar longer to see what happens to them. Look at how they lose volume so that eventually they float in the water and even dissolve! You could also try to clean them with lemon juice.

The citric acid in lemon juice also reacts with the calcium carbonate.

Vinegar to clean

Apart from vinegar with salads, drug stores and supermarkets sell concentrated vinegar for cleaning. It's like the vinegar that you have used in your experiment, but stronger. And it's great for cleaning, for example, those white patches of calcium carbonate that appear on pipes and taps!

4

If they are already sufficiently clean, wash them well with soap and water so that the vinegar stops reacting with them.

The mollusks in the oceans are in danger!

The gas that you have seen during your experiment—carbon dioxide—is also produced in huge quantities by factories. When there is a lot of carbon dioxide in the Earth's atmosphere, it is absorbed by the sea. This makes it more acidic, like vinegar, and some of the calcium carbonate disappears. As you have seen in this experiment, this is bad for the mollusks and other marine creatures with shells because their skeleton dissolves and they can't survive—neither shellfish nor the fish that feed on them.

Eco-friendly surfers

You can see how some small insects skate with great skill over the calm waters of rivers and lakes. These insects, known as Gerridae, glide over the water on four delicate feet, leaving the front pair free to capture their food.

How do they glide over the surface of the water?

What will you need?

- Colander
- Two or three *Gerridae*
- A transparent jar
- Two trays
- Water and dish soap

Experiment

Would you like to find out how Gerridae are able to support themselves above the water? Can they support themselves over any type of water? Try it out!

1 Capture two or three small *Gerridae* and place them in a jar with some water.

2 Grab two large, clean trays. Make sure that there is no grease or oil left over from cooking!

3 Add clean water to one of them, but add a few drops of dish soap to the water in the other, making sure that it does not form bubbles.

THINK LIKE A SCIENTIST

Why do the water striders act differently in the two trays?

These insects are able to glide on the tray that contains no detergent because their feet have very tiny water-repellent hairs that use the surface tension of the water to keep them afloat.

Soap reduces the surface tension of the water; as a result, it cannot hold up the weight of the insects and they sink.

Surface tension is a force created by the water molecules only on the surface. It exists because those molecules act like tiny magnets.

These and other insects use this force to glide over the water in search of food.

Continue investigating

Other examples that are based on water surface tension are capillarity and the use of emulsions (such as mayonnaise).

Capillarity is the ability that a given liquid has to climb spontaneously up a very thin pipe, called a capillary. This is how sap rises from tree roots to their leaves. The thinner the capillaries are, the higher the water can climb. A capillary must be less than one tenth of a millimeter thin.

Mayonnaise is an oil emulsion that remains intact in water thanks to the egg yolk that it contains.

Ecological indicators

What is an ecological indicator? The presence of a given species (in this case, Gerridae) is an unmistakable sign that water is detergent-free. For ecologists, the presence of Gerridae in fresh water is an excellent sign of good water quality.

A very tense record!

The Greeks tested surface tension without even knowing it. They played a game in which opponents skipped stones across the surface of the water. The winner was the contestant who managed to bounce the stone the most times before it sank. The stone skips across the water as a consequence of surface tension, but there are other factors that affect how it bounces. The angle that the stone is thrown at is the most important; about 20 degrees is what works best. Trajectory is also influenced by speed (the greater the better), the shape of the stone (round or flat), and its rate of spin. Perhaps, with this information, you can break the world record, which currently stands at 51 bounces!

4 Place the *Gerridae* in the first tray and observe their behavior. Then move them to the second tray and do the same.

5 Place the insects in a jar with water and return them to their natural habitat.

Mind the waves!

When you're on the beach watching the waves break on the shore, you'll realize that you have never stopped to think about how they are formed. Have you ever considered how water particles make the waves move? Well, here we are going to use a simple experiment to find out—and you don't even have to live near the sea!

What will you need?

- A balloon
- 20 inches (50 cm) length of string
- A stone
- A swimming pool (you can experiment at a smaller scale in your bathtub using a smaller balloon and stone)

Experiment

Would you know how to draw how water particles move and affect the movement of waves? Surely not. But don't worry; after this experiment you will understand how to do just that.

1

Blow up the balloon, knot it, and tie the string around the knot. Make sure that it is securely attached so that it doesn't come undone while the experiment is underway.

2

Tie a stone at the other end of the string, making sure that it is also well tied. The stone should be large enough to act as an anchor for the balloon but not totally sink it.

3

Place the balloon and stone into the water and begin to form waves by moving the water back and forth with your hands. If the balloon does not move, it is submerged too fully in the water and you will need to replace your stone with a lighter stone.

THINK LIKE A SCIENTIST

What happened? Opposite to what we would expect, the balloon starts to revolve around the stone. Why does it do this? Although water in waves appears to move forward, it is in fact water molecules moving up and down in a circular motion. Any object above the waves moves in circles.

Continue investigating

Not all waves are the same, and their shape is dictated by the seafloor and beach. A beach that slopes gently into the sea will produce gentle, low waves. However, a steep incline will result in tall, strong waves. Why not have a look at the waves near where you live or when you visit the beach on vacation, and compare them to waves on other types of beaches.

Are there waves on the bottom of the sea?

Wind is the main cause of waves, causing the water molecules to move in a circular motion. The diameter of this circular motion is at its maximum on the surface of the water and decreases with depth. It also assumes a more elliptical shape as it moves toward the seafloor, by which time it has become barely detectable.

Tsunami: The giant wave

A tsunami occurs when a series of waves that originate deep in the ocean come together and can measure 100 feet (30.5 meters) to the crest. These "superwaves" are caused by massive underwater earthquakes; the ocean floor suddenly drops or rises, displacing huge quantities of water toward the coastline.

Observe how the balloon moves. Did you think that it would move like that? Now what do you think about the movement of water particles in waves?

Shield of protection

"Come on, I have to put sunscreen on you!" How many times have you heard your mother say that as soon as you have arrived at the beach? Well, now you will understand why, because the sun can be very harmful, resulting in very painful burns and other much more dangerous medical conditions. Sunscreen is a genuine protective shield against the sun's rays. Do you want to try it out?

What will you need?

- A magazine
- A sunny day
- Sunscreen

Experiment

Would you like to test how sunscreen works?

1 Remove a page from any magazine; it's even better if it is a full-page multicolored photograph.

2 Spread sunscreen across half of the page, being careful not to tear it.

3 Put the page where it can be exposed to the sun all day long. Choose a spot where it will not get wet or torn.

THINK LIKE A SCIENTIST

Why does sunscreen protect you from the sun's rays?

The light from the sun is a combination of all the colors of the rainbow, and, what's more, some colors that your eyes cannot even see. One is infrared, an invisible light whose presence you feel as the warming sensation from the sun. The other invisible color is ultraviolet. You can't see or feel ultraviolet rays, but they have sufficient energy to destroy particles of ink that color the pictures in your magazine. The worst is that it can destroy parts of your skin, resulting in burns and other medical conditions. Sunscreen allows almost all sunlight to pass but blocks ultraviolet rays, trapping and absorbing its energy so that it doesn't damage your skin.

Continue investigating

If you look carefully, you will see that your parents' sunscreen is different from your own. Normally sunscreen for children offers more protection against ultraviolet rays because, since your skin is younger, it is more sensitive and easier to damage. Repeat your experiment, dividing the magazine page into different sections, leaving one section totally exposed to the sun, another covered with your parents' sunscreen, another covered with your sunscreen, and the last totally covered with another object that doesn't let the sun's light pass, such as a book. Can you see any differences between sections at the end of the day?

Sunglasses

There is another part of the body that is vulnerable to damage from the sun that we must protect well. Can you guess what it is? Exactly, the eyes! But you can't rub sunscreen into them! To properly protect them, you will need a good pair of sunglasses that protect you from invisible ultraviolet rays.

The ozone layer

In the Earth's atmosphere there is a shield that protects your skin by filtering out ultraviolet light: the ozone layer. If this shield did not exist, you would not be able to set foot outside on a sunny day without putting yourself in danger! Years ago scientists discovered that some gases used in aerosol sprays had reached the atmosphere and were harmful to the ozone layer, resulting in a hole the size of Europe, although above Antarctica. Luckily, these sprays are now illegal and the ozone layer seems to be regenerating itself little by little.

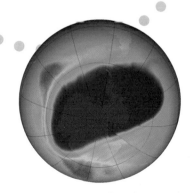

4

Go back in the evening and closely examine the page. The two halves are completely different! The sunscreen has protected the colors from the effects of sunlight.

Dismantling seawater

Do you know what seawater is made of? It is composed of two elements that are normally found as gas but combine to create water: oxygen and hydrogen. And what about the salt? This is also a combination of two elements, sodium and chlorine. Do you want to learn how to "dismantle" seawater and see the hydrogen in the water and the chlorine in the salt with your own eyes? You can even give your friends a lesson on the beach with a plastic cup, two pencils, and a battery!

What will you need?

- Transparent plastic cup
- Seawater or salted water
- Two pencils
- A pencil sharpener
- Scissors
- Copper wire
- Nine-volt (9V) battery
- Modeling clay
- An adult

Experiment

Do you want to know how to "break" seawater and separate its hydrogen and chlorine?

1 Prepare the copper wire at home by cutting it into two pieces that are about a hands' width long. Using the scissors, strip the plastic coating from both ends of the wire until you can see the shiny wire inside. Ask an adult to help you with this.

2 Once you arrive at the beach, fill a plastic cup with seawater and place it on a flat surface so that it does not fall over.

3 Attach the ends of the copper wire to the battery terminals with modeling clay.

THINK LIKE A SCIENTIST

Water consists of millions of tiny particles called water molecules, which in turn are composed of three even smaller particles called atoms: two hydrogen (H) atoms and one oxygen (O) atom. Salt is formed by sodium and chloride atoms.

Connecting the pencils to the battery and placing them in the saltwater produces an electric current, causing many electrons to escape from the battery along the copper wire and through the pencils until they dive into the water. They then frantically swim toward the lead of the other pencil, up the other length of copper wire, and back into the battery. You've made a roller coaster for electrons!

As the electrons travel, they interact with water and salt molecules and their atoms, which separate and then re-form themselves into different structures. It's like when they call out "CHANGE PARTNER!" at a dance. When hydrogen molecules conjoin, they create a gas, and when they encounter a chloride molecule, they rise to the surface side by side, creating these incredibly fun bubbles!

Rockets to the moon

This experiment is similar to how hydrogen is produced on an industrial scale. Factories store hydrogen in enormous containers that is later used, for example, in the combustible fuel tanks of space rockets. The rocket that carried the first astronauts to the moon was powered by a simple mix of hydrogen and oxygen!

Continue investigating

Try repeating this experiment with different amounts of salt, without salt, and using plain tap water or distilled water. You will discover how changing the components will generate fewer or more bubbles. Distilled water does not conduct electricity, so the electrons are unable to travel through it—unless you add salt. However, tap water has other substances dissolved in it that act as conductors and will therefore produce bubbles without the addition of salt... although a lot less than before.

4

Sharpen both ends of both pencils so that the lead is at a point at the top and bottom of each of them.

5

Attach the copper wire to the point of both pencils with some more modeling clay.

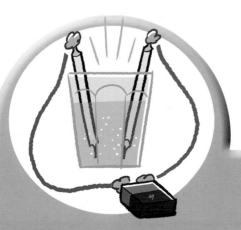

6

Carefully lower the pencils into the cup of water. Then stand back and watch! Bubbles will form around the pencil leads that you have just submerged. They are made of hydrogen and chloride!

I'm going to eat you!

The existence of carnivorous plants and insects is not a myth... it is, as you will see, reality. However, these plants, which live in inaccessible or humid areas, are not dangerous to us. Just because a plant is carnivorous does not mean that it will not atrophy and continue to photosynthesize.

What will you need? ←

- A Venus flytrap
- A magnifying glass (about 4x magnification)
- A toothpick

Experiment

Do you want to closely observe the mechanisms that these plants use to hunt?

1

Get a hold of a Venus flytrap (*Dionaea muscipula*).

2

Look closely (this will be better with a magnifying glass) at the three hairs on each of the two lobes on the interior of the trapping leaves.

3

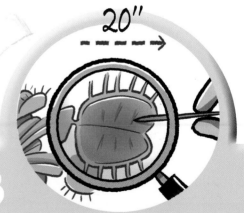

20"

Take your toothpick and first touch only one of the hairs; wait twenty seconds and touch the other. You'll see that nothing will happen.

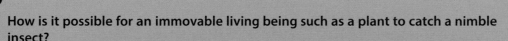

THINK LIKE A SCIENTIST

How is it possible for an immovable living being such as a plant to catch a nimble insect?

Why is it necessary to touch at least two hairs to get a response?

Why do they hunt insects?

The secret of their skill in hunting little insects is the speed with which they can close their leaf traps; however, we still do not know precisely how this mechanism works.

If just one of the plant's hairs is grazed, the plant does not respond; that would be a useless waste of energy because there might not even be an insect.

Plants do not hunt insects for fun or for self-defense; hunting is a way to get nitrogen, since the environment where they live is poor in nitrates. Nitrogen is an essential element for life, since it is used in producing proteins, nucleic acids, and other substances.

Other carnivorous plants

There are other species of plants that use different hunting techniques such as sticky leaves, small adhesive tentacles with which they encircle and immobilize the insect. Some even use leaves that form a bottle shape, attract the insects inside with attractive smells, and then trap them once they are inside.

Species such as *Pinguicula*, *Drosera*, *Nepenthes*, *Sarracenia*, and *Utricularia* are good examples.

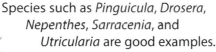

Science fiction carnivore

You're probably seen a movie where giant carnivorous plants trap and devour human beings, such as in Jumanji, The Little Shop of Horrors or The Day of the Triffids. These gigantic species do not exist, although if they did exist, they could probably trap fairly large animals.

2"
--➔

4

Now touch both hairs at the same time, or first one and then the other two seconds later. Surprise! Now the trap works!

Relieve your cough... with a dose of carnivorous plant!

The sticky excretions of some carnivorous plants (such as *Drosera*) are used in medicines because they contain bactericidal substances, expectorants, and antispasmodics. In other words, they can cure a cough.

How much water is in the river?

Water channels carry a volume of water (flow) throughout the year. This can be interrupted or seasonal, as there is a time of year when the flow stops, or ephemeral, when the water does not always flow (streams and watercourses). This fluctuating flow is related to how much water is being fed into its channels. By taking some measurements and a doing a few simple calculations, you can determine the flow of a watercourse.

What will you need?

- Something that floats (a ping-pong ball, small plastic bottle, a stick, a small piece of wood, a cork, etc.)
- Watch or stopwatch
- A tape measure
- A ruler
- A notebook and pencil
- A friend

Experiment

The river flow is the volume of water flowing through its channel at a given time and place. Calculating the speed of the water at a section of the channel will tell you how much water flows by at that point. So grab your tools and get to work!

1 Select an even section of the river, free of large rocks and tree trunks so that the water flows freely, without turbulence or impediment.

2 To determine the speed of the water, use the float method. This consists of timing how long it takes a floating object to travel a given distance downstream (measure the distance with the tape measure).

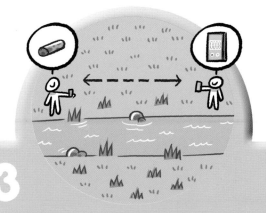

3 One person should be at point A with the floating object and the other at point B with the watch or stopwatch. Measure the time that it takes for the object to travel from point A to point B. We recommend a minimum of 3 measurements, using them to calculate the mean as follows: speed = distance (A-B)/time traveled.

THINK LIKE A SCIENTIST

The float method is a good way to calculate the approximate flow of a water channel, but bear in mind that this does not take other variables into account. The water is not always traveling at the same speed; there is vertical and horizontal friction when the water comes into contact with the banks, riverbed, and air. To avoid errors, scientists use water wheels or ultrasonic measuring devices, allowing them to more accurately determine the speed of the water in each section of the river. Ultrasonic measurements are especially accurate, as they can measure the speed that the water flows with sonic pulses or by the echoes produced by bubbles of water.

Continue investigating

If you would like to make a more precise calculation, take measurements along different sections of the river. As long as there isn't a tributary between your measuring points, the flow should be the same. You will see that there is some variation, so if you want to obtain a single figure, you'll have to calculate the arithmetic mean of the measurements you have made. It's a good idea to measure the flow of the river at different times of the year to accurately record minimum, maximum, and intermediate values, learning more about the behavior of the river in different seasons.

Too much water

Flooding is the natural disaster that claims most lives across the world. An estimated 3.2 million people lost their lives to flooding in the twentieth century, more than half of the total number of people killed in all natural disasters during that period. On many occasions, damage to both humans and property can be avoided by considering the landscape and not constructing dwellings in areas naturally prone to flooding by rivers and heavy rains.

The largest river in the world

The Amazon transports more water than the Mississippi, Nile, and Yangtze combined. The quantity of water that it takes to the Atlantic Ocean is enormous: an annual average of 754,593 feet, rising to 984,252 feet in the rainy season. It transports so much water to the sea that the salinity level of the Atlantic Ocean in the several thousand miles surrounding the river mouth is notably lower. Compare the flow that you have measured to the Amazon... is there a lot of difference?

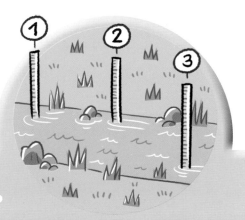

4 Now you have to measure a cross-section of the river, multiplying width by depth, although since the depth is not the same in every section, we recommend that you make different measurements at distinct points and use them to work out a mean depth.
Cross-section area = width x mean depth.

5 Finally, determine the flow of the river by multiplying the results that you obtained through the previous steps:
Flow (m³/s) = water speed (m/s) x cross section (m²).

The time guardian

Want to know what time it is? Easy. You can check a watch or a cell phone. But when you're on the beach, it can sometimes be more difficult to find out because the watch and cell phone are inside a bag, under a mountain of towels so that they don't get ruined by the sand. If you want to surprise your friends, you can make your own sundial. It will take all day... but the next day you will be an authentic time guardian!

What will you need?

- Ten shells
- A permanent marker
- A stone

Experiment

Would you like to make your own sundial?

1

Find ten shells and write the following time on them with your permanent marker: 10, 11, 12, 1, 2, 3, 4, 5, 6, and 7 (representing 10 in the morning until 7 at night).

2

Look for a section of beach open to the sun and far from water and rocks. It's also important that few people pass through, so that when you come back the following day your sundial will still be there.

3

Place a marker in the sand; this will be the center of your clock. Use, for example, a stone or something that you can easily locate later on.

THINK LIKE A SCIENTIST

How does a sundial measure time passing?

The Earth travels through space like a spinning top, turning itself around. It turns round once a day. That is why half of the day you can see the sun, but the other half of the day you can't (night). As you are on the earth it seems as if the sun is moving, just like when you travel in a car it seems as if the world outside is moving.

During its apparent trajectory across the sky, the sun rises over the horizon in the east, producing long shadows early in the morning as it is low in the sky. It then ascends and the shadows move with it until, in summer, it is above you and casts very little shadow. Later it continues its trajectory toward the west and the shadow grows longer on the other side of the stick. The trajectory of the sun will be practically the same the next day, meaning that the shadows will fall on your shells at the same time.

Continue investigating

You can also make a sundial at home, if there is somewhere that is exposed to the sun for many hours each day. You can make it using index cards to mark the hours, a pen as a stick (or "gnomon," as the center stick of a sundial is called), and plasticine to hold the pen in place. Check the accuracy of your sundial every 10 days… you will see that your clock is not as accurate and the shadows are changing! This is because the trajectory of the sun across the sky changes throughout the year.

Sundials

A long time ago, all clocks were sundials. Think about old houses… many of them have sundials built into their facades! And what's more, these sundials are the same as yours: they have a stick and some marker to indicate the time.

4 Exactly on the hour (for example, 10 o'clock), stand at the point that you have marked for the center of your clock. Look where the shadow of your head falls and place the shell with the number 10 written on it in that spot.

5 Repeat the last step on the hour, always placing the shells at the edge of your shadow (your head).

6 Return to the beach the next day. Stand in the center of your watch where your marker is located and look at the shadow of your head to tell the time. If it falls just between two shells, it will be half past the hour.

Science begins at home

Restless air

Wind occurs when air moves horizontally due to changing air pressure in different parts of the world. Where air is warmer and lighter than the air surrounding it, it tends to rise, reducing air pressure. Cold, heavier air tends to travel downward, increasing air pressure. Winds blow from areas of high pressure (anticyclones) to areas of low pressure (cyclones). In this experiment you will use hot and cold water to recreate this process so that the conclusions you reach can equally be applied to the movement of bodies of water in the Earth's oceans.

What will you need?

- Two plastic bottles
- Two plastic tubes
- Two containers
- Two clothespins
- Modeling clay
- Food coloring
- Ice
- Hot water
- Scissors

Experiment

Ask an adult to perform any operations that may be dangerous, and start imitating the movement of the air in the atmosphere.

1 Cut off the top part of two bottles. Make two holes, one above the other, at the same height in both bottles.

2 Cut two tubes to the same length. Insert them into the holes in the two bottles and seal them with modeling clay.

3 Put hot water into one container and ice into the other, and put one bottle into each container. Do this step carefully so that the tubes remain connected to the bottles.

THINK LIKE A SCIENTIST

The heat creates rising currents in the hot bottle and currents that travel downward in the bottle standing in ice. When the clips are removed, the water passes through the bottom tube of the cold bottle and returns through the top tube when it is warmed up. Both winds and ocean currents act in the same way: colder regions move the warmer regions to a lower level.

Continue investigating

In a variant of this experiment you can dip a smaller container filled with colored hot water into a larger container filled with cold water. If you quickly remove the top from the small bottle, you will see that the colored hot water rises toward the surface before sinking slowly lower and mingling with the rest of the water. Hot water is less dense, i.e., it is less heavy and rises toward the surface because it is lighter. It is for this reason that the colored hot water floats above the cold water and only begins to mingle with the cold water when it loses its heat.

A source of energy

Wind power transforms the wind into electricity. This is done by wind turbines, huge windmills 125 or 150 feet [40–50 m] high with propellers up to 75 feet [23 m] in diameter. The wind makes the propeller on the turbine go around, and the rotor on a generator converts this force into electrical energy. On the back there is a type of weather vane that responds to the wind direction.

4 Pinch the tubes shut with clothespins and fill the bottles with different colored water.

5 Remove the clothespins at the same time and watch what happens.

A lethal wind

Hurricanes are huge tropical cyclones that cause very strong winds, enormous waves, tornadoes, and torrential rainfall that can result in floods and landslides. They form over vast areas of warm water and lose power as they reach land. That is why coastal areas suffer extensive damage by tropical cyclones, while inland areas are relatively safe from strong winds.

Quantum leaps

The science of quantum physics is full of mysteries! The smallest of particles can be in different places at the same time, making quantum leaps as they disappear from one place, only to reappear in another. It is a peculiar world that only the best scientists—like you—can see. Do you dare to venture into the universe of quantum physics?

What will you need?

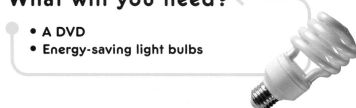

- A DVD
- Energy-saving light bulbs

Experiment

Do you want to see the effect of a quantum leap with your own eyes?

1
Turn on the low-energy light bulb, turn off all other lights, and position yourself as far away as you can from the bulb. The smaller the bulb appears to you, the better you will be able to see the effects of the experiment.

2
Take the DVD and bring the shiny side—that is, the side that does not have any writing or pictures—close to your right eye as if it were an eye patch.

3
Turn your back on the bulb. Tilt the DVD slowly until you can see the bulb reflected in it, as if it were a rearview mirror.

THINK LIKE A SCIENTIST

Why are the shiny-colored lines separated?

Are all of the lines separated by the same distance?

What differences do you notice when you use different types of bulbs?

Low-energy bulbs emit light when tiny particles called electrons inside them fall on top of each other as they journey around inside of atoms. They are thrown by a kind of slide, but... surprise! Instead of sliding down the slide as you would, the upper part of it disappears and mysteriously appears in the lower part! That's a quantum leap! You can see each quantum leap reflected as a color in your DVD, and the colors vary depending on the color of the slide.

The DVD is like a mirror formed by hundreds of microscopically small rays that break up the light. Light from light bulbs is white, but it is the sum of different colored light. If the bulb is an older-type filament bulb, or LED, you will see all of the colors like a rainbow; but, if the bulb is low-energy or fluorescent, you will see the amazing lines that electrons emit when they quantum leap!

What are the stars made of?

You have used the DVD to construct an authentic spectroscope, a scientific apparatus that allows us to observe the colors that make up light. Astronomers use similar spectroscopes to analyze the light from stars and find out what kind of gases they are made of. Every gas has its own unique "signature" of colored rays called a spectrum. When light bulbs emit a white light formed by only a few colors, they consume little energy, and that is why they are called low-energy light bulbs. In older light bulbs, much of this energy is wasted, giving out heat as well as light and therefore using much more electricity than their low-energy counterparts. The latest invention is the LED light, which consumes very little energy but, nevertheless, can emit light containing all colors of the rainbow.

Planet HD189733b

Scientists at NASA have used spectroscopes aboard the Hubble Space Telescope to discover a planet that is blue, like our own, 63 light years away from Earth. Instead of water, the planet has liquid glass heated to 1832°F (1000°C)! They have called it a difficult name to remember: HD189733b

4

Keep the image of the bulb on the right side of the DVD and closely examine the left-hand side of the disc. You will see lines of brilliant colors, separated and caused by the quantum-leaping electrons!

Continue investigating

If you see lampposts in the street that emit a golden-yellow light, they probably contain a gas called sodium. You can observe them with your DVD-spectroscope. If the lamp does contain sodium, you'll see a very bright yellow line separated from the others. Ask for a DVD when you visit a friend and find out whether their lamppost bulbs are low-energy, as if you are a fortune teller. You'll surprise your friend!

The jewels in the crown

Hidden away in some corner of your grandparent's house, there is probably an old silver teaspoon that someone bought as a souvenir or a silver necklace that your grandma bought when she was 20. Silver! It is supposed to be a lovely, shiny precious metal... but this teaspoon or necklace has horrible black marks on it. Surprise everyone by making it as good as new!

Experiment

Are you ready to become a restorer of precious metals?

What will you need?

- A silver object that has become blackened with time (antique jewelry, a piece of cutlery, etc.)
- An aluminum tray (of the disposable type, used for cooking in an oven)
- A mug
- Water
- Salt
- Baking soda
- Disposable gloves
- A tablespoon
- An adult

1 Heat up a mug of water in the microwave on full power for a minute and a half.

2 Take it out carefully (or, even better, ask an adult to help you as you may burn yourself), add two tablespoons of salt and two tablespoons baking soda and stir well.

3 Place the silver object in the aluminum tray.

⚛ THINK LIKE A SCIENTIST

How did the black marks that you have made disappear in your experiment form?

The silver has reacted over many years with a gas present in the air: hydrogen sulfide composed of sulfur and hydrogen. When you place the silver into a receptacle with hot water, aluminum, and baking soda, it produces a chemical reaction that separates the sulfur from the silver, combining with the aluminum in the tray due to the presence of the baking soda. The salt and the hot water help to speed up the process.

Continue investigating

You could reverse this experiment and age a new piece of jewelry so you can later restore to its former shine… although there is a risk that it might go wrong! Place the jewelry in a plastic bag with two recently cooked and halved hard-boiled eggs. Gaseous sulfur from the eggs will react with the silver and darken it!

Professional jewelers

Jewelers use this and other chemical reactions to clean old coins and silver jewelry, gold, or precious stones. Every chemical substance has its distinct properties, which they combine with a given substance to get rid of black marks and return a piece of jewelry to its shining glory.

4

Cover the object with the hot water from the mug and leave it to stand. After a few hours the silver will be totally clean and shiny! Use gloves to remove the silver from the tray.

The Lion of Lydia

If, during your search through your grandma's drawers, you find a coin with the head of a lion pictured on it, you've been very fortunate: this is the Lion of Lydia, the oldest coin in the world. It was minted in silver and gold by the ancient Greeks 2,600 years ago!

Would you like to see DNA?

DNA carries all necessary information to build a living being. DNA contains all of the characteristics that make you unique. Each one of your more than 50 billion cells contains 23 pairs of DNA molecules in the form of chromosomes.

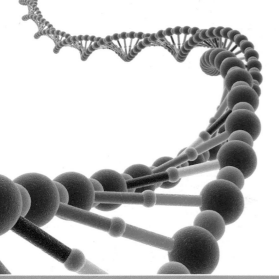

What will you need?

- A biological sample: can be half a banana, a few strawberries, a medium-sized tomato, a small onion, a chicken liver, etc.
- Distilled or mineral water
- 96% proof alcohol (that you must put in the freezer for a few hours beforehand)
- Dish soap
- Table salt
- A bowl
- A blender
- A plastic or glass rod
- A test tube
- A glass
- A syringe
- Fine colander or coffee filter
- Tablespoon
- Ice

Experiment

Do you think that it's impossible to examine microscopic DNA molecules at home? You will find out that it is possible.

1 Fill a glass with 2 tablespoons of distilled or mineral water and add a tablespoon and a half of dish soap and a tablespoon of salt. Place the glass in a bowl full of ice to keep the mixture cold.

2 Cut the biological sample into small pieces and put it in the blender, adding a tablespoon of distilled or mineral water. Blend the contents for 10 to 20 seconds at intermittent intervals.

3 Add your blend, which should have a thick texture, to the glass that you cooled before. Gently stir the mixture for five minutes, ensuring that it does not foam. Then strain the mixture through a colander.

THINK LIKE A SCIENTIST

Remember that DNA is protected inside the nucleus of cells.

What do you think the blender does?

What do the dish soap, salt, and alcohol do?

The blender breaks cell membranes.

The dish soap breaks nucleus membranes, as detergents attack fatty material that forms part of biological membranes.

The salt prevents proteins from binding to the DNA.

The alcohol triggers the DNA while keeping its molecules stretched.

A promising future

This method is refined so that pure DNA can be obtained, from which we can find out the individual that it belongs to, from only a tiny sample such as a drop of saliva! Practical applications are immense in medicine and biology, criminology, or paleontology. It even seems as if the DNA molecule will be the future hard disk!

Jurassic Park is really possible!

DNA samples from fossilized organisms can be used to reconstruct extinct species such as mammoths and dinosaurs.

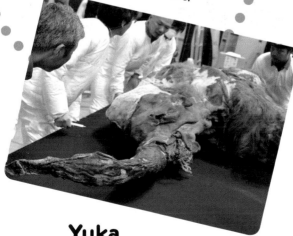

Yuka

In the summer of 2010, scientists found the remains of a baby mammoth frozen in the Siberian ice. They baptized her Yuka. Even though she died some 39,000 years ago, her remains were so well preserved that they contained organic tissues that still held her DNA. Scientists propose separating this DNA in an attempt to clone her, resurrecting a species that died out about 6,000 years ago.

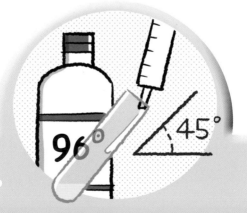

4 Measure 1 teaspoon in your syringe and put it into a test tube. Add 1 teaspoon of very cold 96% proof alcohol, letting it slowly slide down the side of the tube, which must be tilted about 45 degrees until it is floating in the mixture. Allow the tube to rest in an upright position until a cloudy area forms between the two layers.

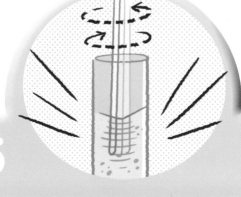

5 Lower the rod in until it reaches the cloudy area and slowly stir for a minute, alternating the direction. You will see a whitish, cottonlike substance form on the rod: congratulations, you have managed to isolate DNA!

Imminent eruption

A volcanic eruption is a discharge of magma, which is formed by molten rock and gases of different types (water vapor, sulfur, nitrogen...). Volcanoes form in this way, and although they can be classified differently, their origins and the way that the magma makes its way to the surface are very similar for all of them. The Earth's upper mantle is normally solid, but there are partially melted areas that contain rocks of lower density than the surrounding rock. The lower density rock tends to rise toward the surface, remaining on the inside of the earth's crust or reaching the surface to form a volcano.

What will you need?

- Red candle wax
- 0.5 liter beaker or a transparent (glass) bowl
- A heat source (hot plate or fire)
- Clean sand
- Cold water
- A spoon
- An adult

Experiment

Do you want to know how the magma rises up from inside the Earth? Follow these steps with the right apparatus and you'll soon understand.

1

Put a piece of red wax about 1 cm thick at the bottom of a transparent bowl or beaker.

2

Ask an adult to help you heat up the bowl or beaker until the wax melts. When the wax has melted completely, remove the bowl or beaker from the heat source and leave it to cool.

3

Add 1 cm of clean sand, forming a uniform layer over the cooled wax.

THINK LIKE A SCIENTIST

How can we explain what happened? What happened to the wax once it melted? And why do you think it happened? What represents each material used in reality?

The sand and water represent layers of the Earth's crust. The wax represents the normally solid upper mantle, which can be partially molten in some areas. In the same way that wax rises because of its lower density relative to the material that surrounds it, magma can rise up into the Earth's crust, sometimes reaching the surface, and form a lava flow.

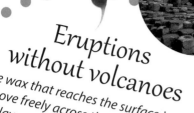

Continue investigating

This model may be related to the theory of plate tectonics. Research the type of plates that cause these eruptions, and search the Internet for photos of landscapes formed by volcanic plateaus.

Eruptions without volcanoes

The wax that reaches the surface is able to move freely across the surface, forming a layer that simulates the so-called "basaltic plateaus" such as those found in Iceland or County Antrim (Northern Ireland), in which enormous volumes of lava did not come from specific volcanoes but from fissures in the crust.

When magma moves, the Earth shakes

Small earthquakes are always being recorded in volcanic zones around the world, but these can worry local people. This is due to the fact that, in the process of magmatic intrusion (ascension), liquids and gases in the magma pressure the oceanic crust, looking for an escape route. This generates a fracture that causes seismic movement. Thanks to these small tremors and other indicators, geologists can anticipate eruptions and warn populations in time to save them.

4 Add the cold water (better chilled in the refrigerator) until the receptacle is three-quarters full. Pour the water into the spoon so that it does not fall directly onto the sand. By doing this, the sand will not be disturbed.

5 Place the bowl or beaker with the wax, sand, and water on the heat source again.

6 You will observe that the wax rises up through the sand and water, as it would move from the Earth's interior to its surface.

The mirror with superpowers

This morning you will have seen yourself in the mirror, just as you do every day when you wake up. What a sleepy-looking face! But have you noticed that all mirrors are not the same? Some mirrors magnify things and are ideal for using while putting on makeup or shaving... you must have at least one mirror like this at home. Find it and you will discover something that nobody else in your house knows... this mirror has superpowers!

What will you need?

- A curved cosmetic or shaving mirror (concave mirror)
- A sheet of black cardstock
- An adult

Experiment

Do you want to see how a mirror can make a hole in a piece of card without even touching it?

1 Take the cardstock and mirror into your yard on a sunny day. With the mirror in one hand, angle it toward the sun. Remember not to look directly at the sun, as this is dangerous.

2 Hold the cardstock in your other hand and position it approximately a palm's length in front of the mirror. Do not block the sunlight, which should be able to reach the mirror.

3 Tilt the mirror, and try moving it closer and further away from the cardstock until you see an image of the sun projected onto it. Then move the cardstock slowly away until the projected image becomes a small dot.

THINK LIKE A SCIENTIST

Where did the heat that scorched a hole in the cardstock come from? Repeat the experiment with a white sheet of paper. Does the same thing happen? Mirrors are normally flat. They reflect light, diverting it so that it seems to come from another direction—from behind. That is why you see yourself when you look into a mirror. Although the image seems real, it isn't... there is nothing behind the mirror. But a concave mirror is very different! If you touch one with the palm of your hand, you will feel that it is curved rather than flat. This shape reflects the light in front of the mirror. The sun concentrates the light, projecting a very realistic image of itself. This image is powerful enough to burn a hole in a sheet of paper! White surfaces are very good at reflecting light. This is why the white sheet of paper does not heat up and catch fire as quickly as the black cardstock. Black surfaces absorb the light and all of its energy, and that is why the black cardstock catches fire more quickly than the white paper. Why do you think that in summer most people wear clothes that are light in color and that houses in the villages with the hottest weather are painted white?

Continue investigating

You can see how real the images that form in a mirror are. If you sit about a foot and a half in front of one, you will see your image reflected upside down. Now touch the point of your nose and begin to move it slowly toward the mirror, with your index finger pointing forward. The image of your hand in the mirror is so real-looking that it will seem as if you are pointing at yourself! It almost appears that you can touch yourself!

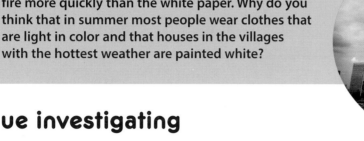

4

Wait patiently for a few minutes, and make sure you have an adult to supervise you. You will see how the bright spot of light begins to smoke. Be careful, because the sun can burn! Its rays have been focused on the cardstock, making a hole right through it!

Mirrors that generate electricity

Similarly, much larger mirrors, as big as buses and grouped in the thousands, can harness the power of the sun to generate electricity and together form thermal solar power stations. Heat is concentrated into a vat of water, causing it to reach boiling point. The steam escapes and drives a special turbine (like a giant fan) that generates electric current as it moves. This electricity is then directed to the plug sockets in your house.

Mind the walkie talkie

If you visit London, watch out for the building they call the Walkie Talkie! The architects did not take into account that the concave mirror that is formed by one side of this glass skyscraper would magnify sunlight. So far it has melted a car's rearview mirror and set fire to a carpet in a nearby hairdresser's shop!

I've run out of glue!

It's the perfect weekend to do some arts and crafts. You've got everything that you need: markers, scissors, colored pieces of paper, some bottlecaps... you're about to start sticking everything together, but oh dear! You've run out of glue. But don't worry, there's a really quick way to make your own!

What will you need?

- A saucepan
- Flour
- Water
- Spoon
- Measuring tablespoon
- An adult

Experiment

Do you want to know how to make homemade glue?

1 Cover the bottom of a saucepan with four or five tablespoons of flour and add a little lukewarm water (not too hot and not too cold).

2 Mix with your hands and add water little by little until it forms a thin, watery paste.

3 With the help of an adult heat the saucepan, stirring it gently as it comes to a boil.

THINK LIKE A SCIENTIST

Flour produced from wheat, as well other foodstuffs such as potatoes and rice, contains a chemical compound called starch. If you could examine it through a strong microscope you would see that it has a very rigid structure, similar to a jungle gym in your local park. When starch dissolves in hot water the reaction forms a paste, which affects this rigid structure: the "jungle gym" is broken.

The paste works as glue because as it cools, its structure becomes more and more rigid until the "jungle gym" is formed again, creating a glue strong enough for paper, cardboard, and wood.

Buildings made with glue

Starch-based glue, made predominantly using rice, was used more than 1,000 years ago in China and Japan to lay bricks and construct buildings, as well as create decorations for women.

The glue that doesn't stick

Glue that you can buy in a store also relies on a chemical reaction for its stickiness: it needs to react when exposed to the air or humidity. That's why it doesn't stick to the inside of its tube. However, when it is out of the tube and comes into contact with humidity and/or the air, a chemical reaction occurs, which means it can stick things together.

4

Leave the paste to cool and you will have perfect glue for your arts and crafts!

Continue investigating

Starch is found not only in wheat flour but can also be found, for example, in rice. Why not try to make homemade glue from rice? Just boil the rice with water until it turns into a paste. Strain out any lumps, and leave it to cool. You've made rice glue!

Keeping feet on the ground

When they fall to the ground, seeds fall in all kinds of different positions. Inside the seed miniature versions of its roots and stem are already formed. So what happens if it falls upside down? Will the stem grow into the ground and the roots up into the air?

What will you need?

- A transparent plastic box, about 12 to 17 inches (30–40 cm) long
- Garden soil or humus
- Water
- Raw bean seeds; you can also use fava beans, chickpeas or corn
- Paper and pencil

Experiment

Do you want to observe how a root always grows downward into the earth while a stem always reaches for the sky?

1 Fill a transparent plastic box with garden soil or humus.

2 Select at least 4 raw bean seeds and bury them at a depth of 1 cm in four different positions, touching the sides of the box so that you can see them from the outside.

3 Water them periodically, but don't let water accumulate at the bottom of the box. Take note of the germination process.

THINK LIKE A SCIENTIST

Why can seeds be sown in different positions?

How do the seeds know in which direction to grow the root and the stem?

Seeds sown in different positions ensure that they will sprout their roots and stems from four different positions. By doing this you can check that as they fall to the ground, the root and stem always grow in the right direction.

The root and stem "know" which direction they need to grow in because they detect the Earth's gravitational field that is stronger toward the interior of the Earth and weaker on the surface. The root is therefore pulled down by gravity, while the stem looks for lower gravity, growing upward toward the surface.

Scientists call this phenomenon gravitropism or geotropism, so that the root demonstrates positive gravitropism while the stem demonstrates negative gravitropism.

Continue investigating

If plants can detect gravity, how will they grow in a spaceship where gravity is practically zero?

On the International Space Station, with the absence of gravity, it has been found that seeds grow in any direction, forming a kind of confused tangle.

Does zero gravity affect humans?

Yes, it affects us a lot. After months in space, astronauts, despite thorough preparation, lose red blood cells, muscle mass, and bone mass. While blood cells and muscle mass can be recovered on the return to Earth, lost bone mass is currently irreversible.

A unique case: The twin astronauts

To better understand the effects of zero gravity on humans, NASA conducted a groundbreaking experiment with two astronauts who are twins, Mark and Scott Kelly. Scott was a resident on the International Space Station for an entire year, while Mark remained on Earth. When this period was over, NASA examined both twins for any changes, as they are identical from a genetic viewpoint. Investigating these differences will hopefully serve to improve treatment of negative effects of weightlessness in the near future.

The bottle that crushes itself

We are surrounded by air, and, although we are not conscious of it, this air occupies a physical space and weighs down on us. In this experiment we are going to use plastic bottles to demonstrate this.

From now on, you can stop saying that this room is empty, this bottle is empty, this glass is empty... they are all filled with air!

What will you need?

- A plastic water bottle with a capacity of 0.25, 0.5, 1, or 1.5 liters
- Boiling water
- Cold tap water
- A funnel

Experiment

Follow these steps with the help of an adult. You will see how air changes its volume due to changes in temperature.

1 Heat water until it boils.

2 Pour the water into the bottle using a funnel. Observe how the bottle wrinkles a little because of the heat.

3 Lightly shake the bottle so that the steam fills the whole bottle, displacing all of the air.

THINK LIKE A SCIENTIST

Why does the bottle crush itself? Why have we emptied out the hot water and then cooled the bottle?

Contact with the hot water increases the temperature of the plastic, which, in turn, heats the air that enters it as the water is emptied. When you close the bottle, the air cools and contracts inside, meaning that air pressure inside becomes lower than the atmospheric pressure. As a result of this difference in air pressure, the bottle collapses in on itself.

Traveling by airplane

When you travel by airplane have you noticed how bottles of water or soft drinks crumple? Although the cabin is pressurized and does not experience the change in atmosphere that occurs due to changes in altitude, there is still a palpable change in air pressure. When closing the bottle while at cruising height, low-pressure air remains inside, crushing the bottle as it descends. You can also see this effect during a car ride, when there is a significant difference in altitude between your city and destination.

My ears have blocked themselves up!

Surely you've experienced a blocked or painful sensation in your eardrums when you're on an airplane or on the road between one city and another that are at significantly different altitudes. This is because the inner ear (specifically the Eustachian tube) does not balance changes in air pressure as we ascend or descend in altitude, producing a vacuum that causes pain or discomfort.

4 Empty out the water and quickly put the lid on.

5 Cool the outside of the bottle with cold water. You will see how it begins to crush itself.

Continue investigating

You can perform a similar experiment by putting a closed empty plastic mineral water bottle in the freezer. Wait for a while before retrieving it, and you'll find it crushed. The air trapped inside drops in pressure in the lower temperature, meaning that the air pressure outside crushes the bottle, reducing the volume of air and balancing internal and external pressures.

Piped electricity

You're at home, there's a storm and suddenly all the power goes out. You can't watch the TV anymore... what a nuisance! The whole block is without electricity... but you can create it with your very own hands! Although you won't be able to create enough electricity to power all of the lights in your house, would you like to learn how to make your own electrical generator?

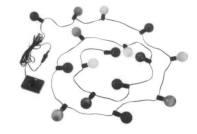

What will you need?

- A long cardboard tube (for example, from an empty paper towel roll)
- Adhesive tape
- A little LED bulb
- One or more magnets
- Copper wire
- Scissors

Experiment

Would you like to light a lamp by converting your movements into electricity?

1

Wind the copper wire tightly around the cardboard tube a hundred times.

2

Use scissors to strip the insulation from the copper wire; then connect the ends of the wire to the light bulb as shown in the illustration.

3

Put the magnet into one end of the tube and carefully close the two ends of the tube by folding over the cardboard and taping it shut.

THINK LIKE A SCIENTIST

Where has the energy that lit the bulb come from?

Try shaking the tube at different speeds. What happens?

For your experiment you have constructed an apparatus that transforms movement into electricity. The electrical cable wrapped around the tube has a few tiny particles inside, called electrons, which can be moved around inside it. It conducts electricity. When you shake the magnets you create a kind of magnetic wave around the tube, pushing the cable's electrons, similar to how ocean waves push surfers.

When arriving at the LED bulb, the movement of electrons (i.e., electricity), becomes light. The stronger you wiggle the cable, the more electrons will move around and the brighter the light bulb will shine.

Continue investigating

Magnets are surrounded with something that you cannot see and yet has power. It's like an invisible arm that grasps and pushes: a magnetic field. Take the two magnets and try to put them together. You will see that sometimes they attract one another forcibly, and other times they repel one another without touching. When they repel one another, you can play cat and mouse with them by pushing one magnet away with the other one without touching it. But watch out! If one of them turns around they will attract one another and stick together.

Magnets also attract and are attracted to other objects that contain iron. Try moving them close to different items in your house and see whether or not the material they are made of contains iron.

Magnetic monopoles

Did you know that nobody has ever found magnets that only repel? Or just attract? Scientists were scouring nature for such magnets 80 years ago, when a scientist named Paul Dirac anticipated that they did not exist. They are called magnetic monopoles, and perhaps you will be the first to discover them! What scientists have managed so far is to produce them in a laboratory. The first magnetic monopole in the world was created by US scientists David Hall and Michael Ray.

Electric power plants

In this experiment you have constructed a tiny electric power plant. Electricity is a form of energy that is transformed into the light from lamps, the heat in a toaster, and the sounds of a radio… But at the same time, the electricity that comes into your house comes from electric power plants, where it was transformed from another form of energy: movement. In some power plants the movement comes from the spinning of turbines by the water that flows down from the mountains; in others, by turning huge windmills. But in all of them the turbines use magnets that are stuck together, like yours but much bigger, that move the electrons and produce electricity.

4

Shut off all the lights so everything is totally dark and shake the tube so that the magnet moves from one end to the other. With every shake you will see the little LED bulb give off a flash of light!

Fruit gets rusty too

Yesterday you had an apple after dinner, but because you had already eaten so much you left a few pieces in the fridge for today.... oh dear! It's turned brown! Do you want to know a trick to prevent this from happening? Try this!

What will you need?

- Three plates and a soup bowl
- An apple
- A lemon
- Water
- Vinegar
- Knife

Experiment

Would you like to learn a cool trick to keep fruit from going bad?

1 Cut up the apple and make four groups of pieces on each of the three plates and the soup bowl.

2 Leave the first group of pieces of apple uncovered on the plate.

3 Pour a few drops of lemon juice over the pieces on the second plate so that the surfaces of the fruit are well covered.

THINK LIKE A SCIENTIST

Which plate has best preserved the fruit? Why?

In the plate that you have left uncovered, you will see that the fruit is covered in brown marks. This is because by cutting the fruit you have broken many of the cells that it is composed of—the "bricks" of all living things. Within these cells are substances that will oxidize when they mix with each other and come into contact with the oxygen in the air. They are transformed into a dark-colored chemical compound called melanin, the same compound that causes your skin to turn brown when sunbathing! To stop this from happening, the fruit must not come into contact with the air. It should be submerged in water or well covered by acids, such as lemon juice. The acid impedes the chemical reaction that produces melanin. Vinegar is also an acid and has the same effect. But apple with vinegar? Not a great taste combination!

Fruits with lots of CHEMISTRY

Bags of chopped fruit that are sold in some supermarkets have also been treated with chemicals so that they do not oxidize. In some cases they are packaged with some kind of acid, such as lemon juice. Others may contain chemical compounds or are vacuum-packed without air so that they do not lose their chemical properties and will not oxidize.

Continue investigating

Try repeating this experiment with different types of fruit such as bananas, pears, oranges, strawberries or pineapples. Does the same thing happen to all of them? The acid taste of some of them will give you a hint!

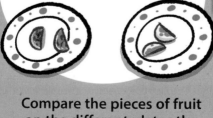

4 Pour a few drops of vinegar over the pieces on the third plate, in the same way that you did the lemon juice.

5 Cover the pieces in the soup bowl completely with water. No part of the apple should be sticking out of the water.

6 Compare the pieces of fruit on the different plates the next day. Which looks nicer, and which tastes better?

Get out of here, microbe!

Microbes, although they can't be seen, are present everywhere (except in sterilized objects). There are many different kinds of microbes, from beneficial to lethal. A microorganism or microbe can be classified as such because it is any form of life that is not visible to the naked eye (bacteria, protozoa, and some algae and fungi).

Do you want to make a cultivable environment, where bacteria and fungi can grow, that will let you check if there are microorganisms in our bodies? Do you think that microorganisms inside the mouth and the hands are the same?

What will you need?

- Sheet of gelatin (stores sell these for thickening gravies)
- Bouillon cube
- Five plastic containers with lids (like Petri dishes)
- A permanent marker
- Cotton swabs
- Soap
- Antibiotic solution
- Water
- Two saucepans
- An adult

Experiment

Are there microbes in our body?
Would you like to see if they are there without using a microscope?

1 Prepare a culture medium where microorganisms can grow, by mixing a sheet of unflavored gelatin with a bouillon cube and 4 cups of water in a pan. Have a grown-up help you warm the mixture over low heat.

2 Sterilize five clear plastic containers with lids. Ideally you can use Petri dishes, which can be purchased at stores that sell laboratory supplies. To sterilize them, leave them in boiling water for five minutes.

3 While the gelatin mixture is still hot, divide it evenly among the sterilized containers and put the lids on quickly. Let them cool and number them from 1 through 5 with a permanent marker, corresponding to the experiments you want to conduct. Do nothing with container 1; it will be your test control.

THINK LIKE A SCIENTIST

Why do you think that it is necessary to boil the containers before you start the experiment?

After carrying out this experiment, do you think that it is important to wash your hands before dinner every day?

Do you think that these microorganisms are beneficial to our bodies?

We have millions of microbes living in our skin and inside our bodies (in our stomachs, intestines, and other organs) that help us to realize some vital bodily functions. This group of microorganisms is called flora, and without it we could not digest food correctly. They also protect us against other more harmful microbes that would use any small wound to enter our body and infect us.

Continue investigating

You can repeat the experiment, but this time use samples from your brothers and sisters or parents, to see if there are any differences. Which of them has the cleanest hands? If you have a microscope you can see these microorganisms by placing a small sample tined with dye on a specimen slide.

Penicillin: The first antibiotic

Alexander Fleming discovered penicillin in 1928, a major advance in medicine that has since saved millions of lives. This penicillin was obtained from yeast (Penicillium), a fungus. We continue to create new antibiotics from other yeasts and bacteria.

You will recognize them by their appearance

Surely you've noticed differences in color, shape, and texture in the different samples you've handled. Scientists are able to identify the different species of bacteria and fungi according to the way they grow. In this way, we can choose what kind of antibiotic needs to be prescribed when we have an infection.

4

Run your hand over a tabletop, rub a cotton swab over your fingers, and wipe it gently on the surface of culture medium 2. Move the swab in a zigzag pattern and rotate the cotton tip so that the entire surface touches the culture medium. Wash your hands with soap and repeat the same steps with container 3.

5

Finally, to see if there are different types of microbes on different parts of your body, rub a cotton swab inside your mouth and repeat the preceding step in container four. You can do the same thing with container 5, but also add the antibiotic solution.

6

Leave the containers in a warm place (95°F/35°C) so that the microbes can grow faster. The growing time is about 48 hours. Every bacterium or fungus that you have "planted" will produce a circular colony that will keep growing over time and merge with the others.

Magic powder

Matter is composed of chemical elements, most of which combine to form compounds. When these chemicals are combined in an orderly manner, they produce crystals (minerals). From a substance normally used as a fertilizer, it is possible to reproduce—in a just few days—the process of formation of minerals on Earth.

What will you need?

- About 10½ oz. (300 g) of ammonium dihydrogen phosphate or ADP (from any drugstore)
- Just over 2 cups (500 ml) of distilled water
- A thermometer
- A pot or saucepan
- A plastic or glass bowl
- Styrofoam box
- Spoon
- An adult

Experiment

Dare to make crystals that will astonish everybody!

1 Pour the 2+ cups (500 ml) of distilled water into a pan, along with the 10½ oz. (300 g) of ammonium dihydrogen phosphate, and heat it up with help from a grown-up.

2 Keep stirring the solution as it heats until all the phosphate has dissolved. Keep heating until the water reaches boiling.

3 Once the solution is dissolved, pour all the contents of the pan into the bowl and put it into the styrofoam box.

THINK LIKE A SCIENTIST

How do you suppose we got our lovely crystals from water and some white ADP powder? What has happened is that when the solution cools down to a certain temperature, it cannot hold so much dissolved ADP, so it expels all the surplus in the form of a solid. If the cooling is slow, the ADP molecules begin to line up in an orderly fashion to form a large crystal; but if the cooling is rapid, all the excess ADP in the solution is expelled quickly, so the ADP crystals do not have time to line up nicely into a single crystal and they form thousands of very tiny crystals.

Continue investigating

You can perform the same experiment, but this time add a little food coloring to give the crystals a new tonality. Furthermore, if you want to enhance the beauty of your crystals, use a crystal that you made before as the nucleus for your new crystal solution. Doing so will make them bigger and bigger. Also try crystallizing in a glass container, rather than a plastic one.

Sugar crystals

Crystallization is used in manufacturing as a way to obtain pure substances dissolved in a liquid. For example, sugar cannot be obtained by filtering or distilling sugarcane juice, given that the temperature at which water boils is much higher than the temperature at which the sugar oxidates. Thus, the only way to obtain the finished product is by crystallizing the solution.

The King of the crystals

Diamonds are the most beautiful and valuable minerals in the world. To form, they need to be heated to 1832°F (1000°C) and some 50 kilobars of pressure (equivalent to 50,000 times the atmospheric pressure of the Earth), so you can't make them at home. The conditions (pressure and temperature) that they require to form are found approximately 93 miles (150 km) underneath the surface of our planet.

4 Cover the bowl and the styrofoam box tightly. If the box does not seal tightly, put tape all around the cover. If you are using a plastic container, let the solution cool for about five minutes to about 150–167°F (65–75°C) before pouring it out, so that the container does not warp from the heat.

5 After three days, remove the cover from the box and the bowl, and you will be amazed at what you see.

Would you like to see the sound of your voice?

Surely you've seen many things during your life, but there's one thing that you have probably never seen, although it is all around you... sound! Yes, you can also see sound, albeit indirectly. And every sound has its own shape. In this experiment you will construct an apparatus so that, besides hearing sounds with your own ears, you will see them with your own eyes.

What will you need?

- A balloon
- Adhesive tape
- A small mirror
- A flashlight
- Modeling clay
- An empty soup can open at both ends

Experiment

Would you like to see what shape your voice is?

1 Cover one of the open ends of the soup can with the balloon as if it were a drum. Secure with adhesive tape.

2 Affix the small mirror to the balloon with modeling clay halfway between the center and edge of the circle.

3 Illuminate the mirror with the flashlight. This will cause light to reflect off the mirror at a certain angle: direct it toward the wall. Try to make the point of light on the wall as bright and small as possible.

THINK LIKE A SCIENTIST

Why does the point of light on the wall move?

What happens if you sing more quietly or loudly?

Sound occurs when we make the air vibrate. We do this with our voice by moving a group of muscles that form a membrane inside of our throats: the vocal cords. As they move, the air moves backward and forward repeatedly and very quickly. It happens so quickly that if you sing a C sharp, the air vibrates more than 500 times a second. These up and down movements in the air, or sound waves, travel to and arrive at your eardrums, membranes that vibrate like the balloon in your experiment. These in turn move three tiny bones that send a message to your brain, which thinks… music!

In your experiment the sound waves of your voice move the rubber membrane and make the mirror vibrate. You can't see these vibrations, but when you reflect a ray of light onto the wall, these small movements are amplified and you are able to see them with your own eyes. The louder you sing the more air your vocal cords vibrate, the more the mirror moves, and, as a result, the more the point of light reflected on the wall moves.

You've become a sound engineer!

Professional singers record their songs in sophisticated music studios, equipped with the most complicated apparatus that you can imagine, covered all over with buttons. But, fundamentally, they do something very similar to what you have accomplished with your soup can. Studio microphones have a very thin membrane, like the rubber of a balloon, which the voice vibrates. These vibrations move small magnets that convert them into electrical currents. These currents arrive at a computer and are transferred into images so that sound technicians can work with them more easily. By doing so, they can delete, cut and paste sections of a song as if they were doing tricks.

25,000 vibrations every second!

The Brazilian singer Georgia Brown holds a Guinness World Record for the highest note sung in the world. She can sing a C10… a note that you cannot even hear! She is the person who is able to make her vocal cords vibrate the most: 25,000 vibrations every second!

GEORGIA BROWN

4

Turn off the lights in the room and talk and sing into the open end of the soup can, as if it were a microphone. Look at the light on the wall. What's happening to it?

Continue investigating

It is not only sound that will make the point of light move. Place the soup can on top of a table and hold it in place with two books. Slap the table twice, or jump up and down on the floor. You will see that this also makes the point of light move. Vibrations are transmitted not only through the air but also by solid materials. Earthquakes are detected and measured in a similar way using a seismograph. This has a needle that amplifies vibrations in the ground and converts them into a chart so that we can study them more closely.

An egg fried cold!

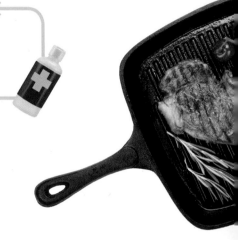

If you think that you need a hot pan to fry an egg, then you are very wrong. You can fry an egg without this, frying it "cold" on a simple plate, as if it were a magic trick. Do you want to know how?

What will you need?
- A soup bowl or dish
- An egg
- Rubbing alcohol (96%)
- A fork

Experiment

Do you want to learn how to fry an egg without heating it?

1 Put the egg in a dish or soup bowl, the darker in color the better so that you can see the egg "fry."

2 Pour the medicinal alcohol over the egg little by little, so that it comes into contact with the egg white.

3 Stir the egg white with a fork while you add the alcohol, without beating the egg; leave it to stand for 30 minutes.

THINK LIKE A SCIENTIST

Why has the egg fried without being heated up?

If you could observe the white of an egg under a very powerful microscope, you would notice that it contains large quantities of very small strands: proteins. When the egg is raw, these proteins are "wrinkled." Each protein is stuck to itself, like a piece of adhesive tape does when you fold it. But when these proteins are heated up in the pan they lose this shape, the wrinkles disappear, and the proteins become like threads in a shirt, forming white, consistent tissue. Scientists call these "denatured" proteins.

But you haven't heated the egg, you've only added alcohol to it. The alcohol has the same effect on the egg proteins, straightening out their wrinkles and transforming them into long threads, giving the egg white its typical white color and the consistency of a fried egg—although it is not edible.

A plate of denatured proteins, please!

If the egg proteins are wrinkled when they reach your stomach, meaning you have eaten the egg raw, it can be difficult to digest and make you feel ill. The same thing happens with proteins in other types of foods, such as meat and fish. Nonetheless, if you eat them as large threads, or denatured proteins, your stomach will be able to digest them easily and your body can make use of them to build your strength. This is why we cook many foods; warming them up allows the wrinkles in the proteins to straighten, and we can better digest them.

Straight hair or wavy hair

Your hair and your nails contain a protein called keratin. The extent to which the keratin "wrinkles" determines the appearance of your hair as it grows, making it curly or straight.

4

30 minutes later you will have an egg white that is consistent and white, just as it is when you fry an egg: there you have it, an egg fried cold! But don't eat it… it's not edible!

Continue investigating

Milk also contains many proteins called caseins. These proteins can be denatured using an acid such as that contained in lemon juice or vinegar. Mix lemon juice or vinegar in a glass with some milk. You will see a solid white thing form on the bottom of the glass. There are proteins, which have "unraveled" as they separate from the water within the milk and fall to the bottom of the glass. Pour the milk through a colander and you will better see this effect. Did you know that this is how you get cheese?

The jumping egg

P lace a raw egg inside a glass full of vinegar and see what happens. In this experiment the shell of the egg reacts to the vinegar, transforming itself as much as the egg white does... the result will surprise you!

What will you need?

- An egg
- A transparent glass jar
- White or wine vinegar
- Water

Experiment

Do you want to transform a brittle egg into a bouncing "rubber" ball?

1

Select an egg from the carton.

2

Find a glass jar, place the egg inside without breaking it, and fill the jar with vinegar.

3

The next day replace the vinegar with fresh vinegar.

THINK LIKE A SCIENTIST

What happened to the eggshell?

Why has the egg white hardened?

Has the yolk changed at all?

The eggshell is basically composed of calcium carbonate, like our bones. Acid in the vinegar reacts with calcium carbonate and dissolves, releasing carbon dioxide bubbles.

Once the egg is dissolved, the egg white cannot break out because it is enveloped in a fine protective but semipermeable layer that is unaffected by the vinegar. This layer lets the vinegar pass, which reacts with the white in a similar way to when it is fried. The "coagulated" egg white displays an elastic behavior, permitting the egg to bounce like a ball. The inner section of the white does not undergo this change, as the vinegar does not penetrate this far.

Also note how the egg has increased in size as a result of the vinegar that it has absorbed.

Continue investigating

As you have seen, an egg is not totally isolated from the exterior by its shell.

Consider that if the egg has been fertilized there would be a chick inside that needs to develop as it grows. It will be sustained by the egg white and yolk, but in addition, it will also need oxygen to breathe. The oxygen it requires penetrates the microscopic pores in the shell and the thin layer that surrounds the white. These pores are where the vinegar has passed, facilitating the changes that you have observed.

Eggs for all tastes!

Eggs are a food very rich in protein and fat. By far the most commonly eaten are chicken eggs, but duck, goose, small quail and giant ostrich eggs, which weigh more than 2 pounds, are also consumed. However the most sought-after are eggs from certain species of fish such as sturgeon, which provide us with very fine caviar.

The art of the egg white

The egg white has been used in paint because of its power to bind. This type of artistic technique was widely used during the Romanesque and the Gothic periods and is known as "tempera paint" or simply "tempera."

4

Wait for another day to pass and take the egg out of the jar. Wash it with water. Let it drop a few inches above a hard surface and watch what happens.

The multicolored column

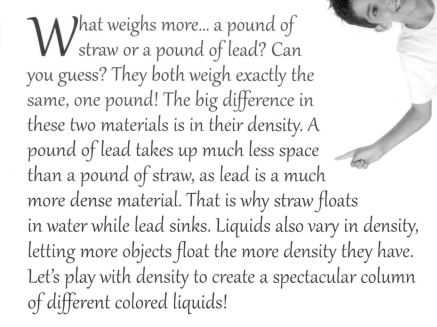

What weighs more... a pound of straw or a pound of lead? Can you guess? They both weigh exactly the same, one pound! The big difference in these two materials is in their density. A pound of lead takes up much less space than a pound of straw, as lead is a much more dense material. That is why straw floats in water while lead sinks. Liquids also vary in density, letting more objects float the more density they have. Let's play with density to create a spectacular column of different colored liquids!

Experiment

What will you need?

- Two small glasses and one tall one
- A syringe
- A variety of food colorings
- Honey
- Corn syrup
- Liquid dish soap
- Water
- Olive or sunflower oil
- Rubbing alcohol
- Spoon

Do you have a steady pulse? Prepare yourself to create a beautiful column of multicolored liquids.

1 Put water and alcohol in two different glasses and add a few drops of different colored dye to each one. Try not to repeat the colors of the other liquids.

2 Spoon a little honey into the tall glass, more or less 2.5 inches (1 cm) from the bottom.

3 Add your other liquids to the tall glass in the following order: corn syrup, dish soap, colored water, olive oil, and colored alcohol.

THINK LIKE A SCIENTIST

What happens if you change the order of the liquids as you mix them?

And what happens if you stir the contents? How do the liquids reorder themselves?

Something is denser than something else if it weighs more but has the same volume. Which do you think is more dense, oil or water? It seems as if the oil is denser because it is more viscous, but it's really the water that's denser. As less dense materials float on top of more dense materials, you can prove this by pouring a few drops of oil into water. You'll see that they float.

You have used liquids with different densities in this experiment in a way that the lower-density liquids float on higher-density liquids. In this way your column of colors has been ordered from higher-density liquids, which remain at the bottom, to low-density liquids, which float to the top. If you pour the liquids in a different order you'll see they form a mix of colors. Leave them to rest a while, and the colors will settle as they were before.

Rising and sinking

Gases also arrange themselves in the air in such a way that the ones of lesser density rise higher than the ones of greater density. This is precisely the reason why balloons filled with helium move upward. Helium is a gas that weighs less than the oxygen and nitrogen that surround us. As a result, if you let go of the balloon, it will take off in search of its place in the column of different densities overhead.

Submarines also can rise and sink beneath the water by using differences in density. They have tanks of compressed air where the air is under so much pressure that its density is the same as that of the water. But if this air is released into a chamber, a type of balloon that can expand, its density decreases and the submarine rises.

The most dense material in the world

Neutron stars are objects in the universe that are unbelievably dense. They aren't very big, normally measuring a few kilometers across. But a piece of a neutron star the same size as a sugar cube would weigh as much as all of the people in the world together!

4

Use the syringe so that they fall little by little along the sides of the glass, making sure they don't mix. You have created a beautiful multicolored column!

Continue investigating

You can find out how dense each liquid is by weighing the same volume of each one. Fill a glass with 16.9 fluid ounces of one of the liquids, measuring with the syringe. Weigh on a kitchen scale and make a note of the weight in grams. Divide the weight by 16.9 to work out the density. Repeat this calculation for each liquid and order them according to density. Are they in the same order as when you did your experiment? You could also add small solid objects of different materials to your column to observe where they settle to know their density. You can try with a wooden toothpick, a nail, an ice cube… notice that the ice cube does not have the same density as water!

Yum! Cheese!

Cheese, when it comes down to it, is no more than a way to keep milk over a long period of time. Long-lasting cheeses are made by fermented milk, thanks to certain species of bacteria or yeast. Milk is produced by cows, goats, sheep, and buffaloes, and there are so many varieties of cheese.

Contrary to milk, cheese does not contain lactose, which some adults cannot digest.

What will you need?

- 1/2 gallon (2 L) pasteurized whole milk
- 3 ounces (90 ml) recently squeezed lemon juice
- A teaspoon of salt
- A saucepan
- A colander
- A cheese towel
- A mold (optional)
- A spoon
- An adult

Experiment

Do you want to learn how to make fresh cheese?

1 With the help of an adult, put the milk into a saucepan and heat it over low heat until small bubbles start to form around the sides of the saucepan.

2 Carefully take the saucepan off the heat and leave it rest for about 20 minutes.

3 Add about 3 ounces (90 ml) of lemon juice and wait for 10 more minutes. Heat the milk again until it separates, add a teaspoon of salt, and stir.

THINK LIKE A SCIENTIST

Why must fresh milk be used?

What does the lemon juice do? And the salt?

You must use fresh milk because sterilized milk is altered by a process that makes it more long-lasting.

The lemon juice contains an acid, which, like all acids, separates the milk and causes the proteins to precipitate.

Salt is used to give additional flavor and make the cheese last longer.

Continue investigating

If you want to make different varieties of fresh cheese you can add yogurt or cream to the milk, resulting in a more creamy cheese.

More than 4,000 years eating yogurt

Yogurt is another example of a lactose derivative obtained by bacterial fermentation. It was discovered by the Thracians, who lived in what is now Bulgaria more than 4,000 years ago. Their kefir is similar to yogurt, but its manufacture involves both a bacterium and yeast.

4

Cover a large colander with a cheese towel and pour in the contents of the saucepan. Wait for the liquid (whey) to strain out. Finally, close the towel and squeeze its contents to get rid of any remaining whey. Place the fresh cheese into a mold to give it the desired shape and keep it in the refrigerator.

10,000 years of cheese!

It is believed that cheese began to be manufactured shortly after sheep were domesticated, about 8,000 or 9,000 years before the present day. Consequently the first cheese would have been made from sheep's milk about 10,000 years ago. About 20 million tons of cheese are currently produced annually worldwide. Greece is the country with the largest consumption of cheese, with an average of nearly 59½ lbs (27 kg) per person per year.

Science in the park

Permeables compete

P ermeability is the speed at which a fluid can pass through the pores of a solid material. If the grade of permeability in a soil is high, then water can easily penetrate. If, on the other hand, the permeability is low, rainwater tends to remain on or run off the surface if the terrain is inclined. In this experiment you will test the permeability of three different soils and find out how water is absorbed by soil at different rhythms, primarily depending on the measurement of its components.

What will you need?

- 3 plastic bottles (1.5 or 2 L)
- A knife or scissors to cut the bottles
- Samples of three local soils or artificial soils prepared with gravel, sand, and clay
- 3 glasses of the same size to pour water into the soil
- Small pieces of fabric and rope (or rubber bands) to retain the soils in their funnels
- Stopwatch or watch
- Water
- Ruler

Experiment

Are you ready for the competition? Which soil do you think will win?

1 Gather three different soil samples (or mix them yourself): one rich in clays, one rich in sand, and another that contains larger pieces of stone or round rocks.

2 Make three funnels by cutting the three plastic bottles in half. Mark about 3 inches (8 cm) up from the neck of each bottle (flush with the soil) and another at 5 inches (12 cm) for the water.

3 Fix pieces of cloth over the mouth of each bottle by tying them to the necks so that the soil cannot escape. Place the funnels inside the other halves of the bottles so that they are suspended above the bottom.

 ## THINK LIKE A SCIENTIST

Which is the most permeable out of the three soils? Which soil lets the water pass more easily? Why do you think that some soils let water pass through more easily?

Large-grained soils with many gaps let water pass through more quickly. Those with smaller grains and less space in between let water pass through more slowly, since it does not pass easily through these narrows gaps. If a soil is made of very fine materials (silts and clays), then the space between grains is so small that water can barely pass through and the soil becomes waterlogged.

Are all soils right for a soccer field?

If you intended to build a soccer field, what kind of soil would you choose: one that lets water quickly pass or one that retains it? A soccer field needs to drain quickly, otherwise it would flood during a storm. It is very difficult to find a natural soil suitable to build a soccer field. Normally the soil is made artificially by mixing clay and one or two layers of sand.

Not even a drop filtered!

It is vital to consider the permeability of a site before selecting it as a waste dump, as fluids generated as waste decomposes cannot filter through to the subsoil. This avoids contamination of the water aquifers, which are so important to maintain a clean water supply for many communities.

4

Fill each funnel up to the mark (without flattening it) with your soil samples. Pour water into each funnel until the samples are saturated. Once they are saturated, pour out any excess water and empty the glasses.

5

Fill another three funnels with water, and, as you start the stopwatch, fill each funnel with water up to the mark. Add more water to the funnels as it is filtered through, trying to keep the level as close to your mark as possible.

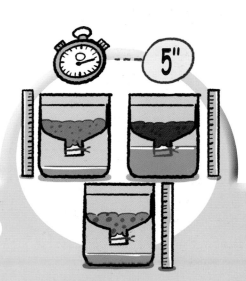

6

After five minutes have passed, stop adding water and measure how much has filtered through the funnel in that time.

Don't be heavy!

I weigh more than you! No, I weigh more than you, I'm the tallest! No, me! Do you want to find out for sure who out of your friends and yourself weigh the most? If you're in the park and there is a spring rider toy such as a horse, you have the perfect set of scales to find out!

What will you need?

- A spring rider toy at a park
- A stopwatch or watch
- A notebook and pencil
- One or more friends

Experiment

Would you like to find out who is the heaviest?

1

Ask one of your friends to sit on the spring rider. It needs to have a spring underneath, enabling it to move backward and forward.

1-2-3-4-5-6-7-8...

2

Ask your friend to ride it for a minute, counting how many times it moves backward and forward in this minute. Write this down. Consider that no matter what force is applied, the number of swings remains more or less the same.

SARA: 26
TOMÁS: 23
MERCEDES: 42
ALBERTO: 17
ANA: 38

3

Repeat the experiment with as many friends as you like, including yourself, and record how many backward and forward swings in a minute happen for each person.

THINK LIKE A SCIENTIST

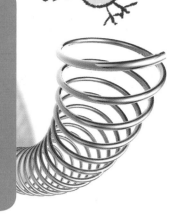

What does the number of oscillations that the spring rider makes depend on? Can you make it go faster and slower on your own?

When you are riding the spring rider and you lean forward at each tilt, you stretch the spring underneath the toy. But the spring doesn't like being stretched, exerting force to return to its natural position and consequently tilting backward slightly. This force depends on your weight and how much you stretch the spring, meaning that the toy moves backward and forward at a fixed rate depending on your weight. If you move according to this rhythm, called "in resonance" with the spring, you will move further forward and further backward. But as much as you try, you'll see that you can't change that rhythm... because it is dictated by your weight!

Do you fancy a glass of warm milk?

Water is made of tiny particles called molecules that are like balls joined together by invisible springs. The same thing happens to them as when you are on the spring rider: they cannot swing either way, more quickly or slower. They have their own rhythm. If you move them at just this rhythm, the molecules move backward and forward more and more... and they warm up. This is exactly what a microwave does with water: it emits waves that push the water particles just at the right rhythm, "in resonance" with each other so that they heat up.

Clocks with springs

The spring was invented in 1660 by an Englishman named Robert Hooke. They enabled the first wristwatches to be manufactured, which used the rhythm inherent in springs. Until then, clocks had used something similar to park swings to keep time: a pendulum, a weight that swung from side to side at a constant rhythm.

Continue investigating

Try the same experiment with a swing. Count the amount of time that it swings back and forth in one minute with various friends. Does it depend on their weight? There is no spring applying force, and the time it takes to move back and forth is always the same, irrespective of weight.

4+

Reorder your list so that you have the person who makes the less backward and forward swings first and the person who makes the most last. You have ordered your friends by weight: the first on the list is the heaviest!

Speedboat!

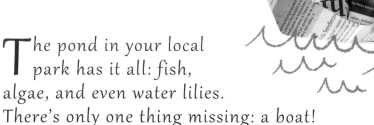

The pond in your local park has it all: fish, algae, and even water lilies. There's only one thing missing: a boat!

Do you want to learn how to make a speedboat that moves across the pond on its own? It's not hard; just follow the steps in this simple experiment.

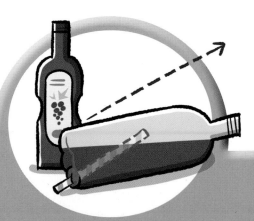

What will you need?

- A plastic bottle
- A straw
- Baking soda
- A tablespoon
- Scissors
- Modeling clay
- A paper towel
- Vinegar

Experiment

Would you like to build a speedboat?

1 Make a small hole in the base of a plastic bottle, near the circumference, using a scissor.

2 Insert a straw into the hole until only a small piece is sticking out, then put a little modeling clay around it to close the hole.

3 Fill the bottle three-quarters full with vinegar and angle it so that the straw is inside the vinegar that is inside the bottle.

THINK LIKE A SCIENTIST

Why does the bottle move on its own?

When the paper towel bundle soaked in vinegar comes into contact with the baking soda, it triggers a chemical reaction. In this reaction the baking soda combines with the acetic acid in the vinegar to produce a gas, carbon dioxide. This gas fills up the whole bottle until it comes out through the straw, propelling the bottle in the opposite direction in which the gas comes out.

Continue investigating

Your speedboat will not move itself for very long because the chemical reaction that the gas produces will cease as soon as all of the baking soda has combined with the vinegar. You could try to design super speedboats using packets of baking soda wrapped in thicker paper or other different types of paper so that the gas is produced in various phases, or by using more vinegar at the start of the experiment.

Into the stratosphere!

Proceed with caution, because making homemade rockets and boats in this way can be addictive. In 2011 a group of enthusiasts perfected this to such an extent that they successfully launched their rocket, Qu8k, into the stratosphere, some 18 miles (30 km) up in the sky!

Full speed ahead!

Rockets use the push that gases provide to rise into the sky, leave the Earth's atmosphere, and travel into space. These gases produce chemical reactions similar to those that you have created inside your bottle, only millions of times more powerful!

4 Put five or six tablespoons of baking soda in a paper towel and wrap it up as if it were a candy.

5 Push the paper with baking soda into the bottle, making sure that it does not spill out, and quickly screw on the lid.

6 Put the bottle into the pond immediately. It will begin to move like a real speedboat.

Who lives here?

There are many more species of birds (more than 10,000) than mammals (less than 5,500). Nevertheless, they are not very familiar to human beings. Would you like to find out a little more? We suggest that you build a bird feeder to help us observe its diet and lifestyle. By doing so, you will learn to identify distinct species and conduct yourself like an experienced naturalist.

What will you need?

- A transparent plastic bottle
- Scissors
- A clay flowerpot
- A rope
- Birdseed
- Gelatin
- Water
- Honey or molasses
- Guide to regional birds
- 2 sticks

Experiment

Do you want to learn how real naturalists can identify bird species that live in a given area? We can do this in a corner of the city; choose a park with trees near your house and let the adventure begin.

1 Find an empty plastic bottle and cut the neck at a distance of about 2 inches (5 cm) from the lid. Also make a hole in the middle of the bottom of the bottle and small slits in the lower part of the bottle, where the birds will be able to take the food from.

2 Thread a piece of rope through the hole in the bottom and tie two sticks together with the rope in the form of a cross. The birds will be able to land on these sticks.

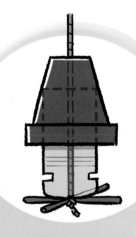

3 Get a clay flowerpot, the kind that has a hole in the bottom, and pass the rope through the hole in the bottom of the flowerpot so that it sits like a hat on top of the bottle. This will protect the seeds from water and the birds from the sun.

THINK LIKE A SCIENTIST

Do you think that you will be able to see the same birds all year round?

What are the most important characteristics to consider when classifying birds?

Many bird species are migratory—that is, they travel hundreds of miles during changes in the seasons looking for more favorable weather conditions. Carry out the same experiment at different times of the year and record the different species you see in a notebook. By doing so, you will know which species remain in the city all year round and which species migrate.

To be able to identify different species you will need to bear in mind their size, the shape of their beaks, and, above all, the color of their plumage. Note that many species are sexually dimorphic—that is, males and females are different colors.

Guardians of the airports

The peregrine falcon is the fastest animal in the world, reaching more than 186 miles per hour in full flight. Given its unbeatable flight speed and easy domestication, it has been used to hunt other birds since antiquity. There are still airports on every continent that use them to keep other birds such as gulls away from aircraft, preventing crashes at landing and takeoff.

Continue investigating

The birds that you attract to your feeder will be granivores (they eat seeds). If you are interested in seeing different types of birds, you will have to change the contents of your feeder. You can make one with insects (the so-called "lesser mealworm") or fruit and see what happens. Compare the results!

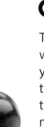

4 Now you are able to fill the bottle with food. Since it is transparent, you will see when the seeds run out and need replenishing.

BIRDSEED
WATER
GELATIN
HONEY

5 One example of bird food could be a mixture of birdseed, water, gelatin, and honey or molasses. Make it at home with hot water and mix the ingredients together thoroughly.

6 Now you are ready to observe the birds in your city. Hang the feeder in a tree in the park and observe the birds that come to feed. You can use a guide to regional birds to identify the most common species.

Make your own water filter

When we drink tap water at home we don't worry that it will make us ill, as we are sure that it has already been purified in a water treatment plant. The purification processes that these plants use are much more complicated that those that you will create here, but you will see how with substances that are easy to come by, such as sand and charcoal, you can create your own treatment system and clean really dirty water. Bear in mind that although the water is transparent, you should not drink it, as the filter does not eliminate bacteria and is still not potable.

What will you need?

- A transparent plastic bottle
- A glass or mug (to make dirty water in)
- A transparent glass (to catch the filtered water)
- Sand
- Medium gravel
- Coarse gravel
- Activated charcoal
- Tablespoon
- Scissors
- Absorbent cotton
- Food coloring
- Soil and grass
- An iced lollipop stick
- Water
- An adult

Experiment

Have you ever wondered how water is purified before it arrives at your house?
Here you will make a simple filtration system that will answer your questions.

1 First create some dirty water by filling a glass or mug three quarters full with water. Add a drop of food coloring to the water, followed by a tablespoon of soil and grass from the garden. Mix everything up with the iced lollipop stick.

2 Cut the bottom of the bottle out.

3 With points of the scissor blades, make some holes in the plastic bottle lid. Ask an adult to help you with this.

THINK LIKE A SCIENTIST

Would you be able to explain what cleaning effects the different layers in your bottle have had? How have they cleaned the water?

The gravel and sand grains group together, leaving only small spaces between them. Since there was no space for the soil or grass to pass through the sand grains, the layers of material have acted as a filter, retaining the solids in the dirty water in suspension but allowing the fluid to pass through their pores. The smaller the pores, the better the material retains solids, and that is why the sand retains better than the gravel. The activated carbon is an absorbent material as well as a filter, it is able to retain small natural, organic particles on its surface (in this case, the coloring).

Continue investigating

Does the filter always work? You will observe how, after it has been used a few times, there will come a moment when there is so much material adhered to the surface of the charcoal that it is unable to eliminate more coloring. But is this layer of carbon really necessary? You could check the absorbent power of charcoal by trying this experiment without the layer of this product. You will observe how, although your filter retains the particles in suspension, it does not eliminate the color or smell of the water.

The filter in my home

Home water filters usually employ activated carbon obtained from mineral coal, of tar or anthracite type, although filters made from coconut shell extracts also exist. The same filters are also used to keep water clean in fish tanks and aquariums.

Aquifers, nature's filters

Aquifers have a given capacity to purify groundwater that can be better or worse depending on the type of rock and other characteristics. Contaminating substances are carried along with the water through subsoil particles, being filtered, dispersed, and undergoing other degrading chemical or biological processes. Water from natural sources tends to be cleaner and taste better than surface water.

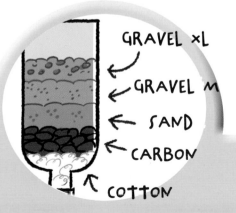

4 Turn the bottle upside down so that you can first put an absorbent cotton layer, followed by the other materials in this order: charcoal, sand, medium gravel, coarse gravel. The thickness of each layer will depend on the size of your bottle and the quality of the filter that you wish to obtain. Thicker layers will produce better filtration.

GRAVEL xL
GRAVEL M
SAND
CARBON
COTTON

5 Pour the dirty water little by little into the upper part of the bottle, making sure that you have placed a transparent glass underneath to catch the water. Be patient, as the first drops of purified water can take some time to emerge.

6 Pick up the filtered water and compare it to the dirty water you initially used.

The Pendulum of the brave

A ttention: experiment for brave people only! Do you know what energy is? It is the ability to do something. If you have a lot of energy, you can do many things. Objects may also have energy and have the ability to do things—for example, move themselves.

Can I tell you a secret about energy? It is always retained! If you are brave, you can rely on the conservation of energy to carry out this experiment.

What will you need?

- A swing
- A backpack full of things
- A rope

Experiment

Do you dare to surprise your friends with this test of bravery?

1 Load a backpack with as much weight as you can: books, notebooks, pencil cases, afternoon snacks… everything.

2 Place the backpack on the seat of a swing, as if it were about to swing, firmly tying it in place with a rope so that it doesn't fall off.

3 Pull the backpack backward by lifting the swing slowly upward, as if it were a small child on the swing. Lift it up until it reaches your nose.

THINK LIKE A SCIENTIST

Why doesn't the backpack arrive at your nose?

When you lift the backpack up to your nose you give it energy. This is called potential energy. You have lifted it up and it will move if you let it go. As it falls it gains speed, reaching its maximum speed when it reaches the bottom of its swing, when all of the potential energy has been converted into the energy of motion—an energy that is conserved as it drops. When it begins its upward trajectory again, its maximum speed drops and it swings up toward your nose once again. How close did it get? It will rise according to the potential energy that you provided as you released it, because remember the secret: energy is retained! It can't go any higher and hit you on the nose because nothing has given it the energy to do so.

Let the show begin!

Have you ever been to the circus? You will find the tallest swings you can imagine there: trapezes. Some of them are nearly 40 feet up in the air, and the trapeze artists perform pirouettes in the air as they jump from one trapeze to the other.

Rollercoasters

Rollercoasters in theme parks take advantage of energy conservation to make all of those loops and spectacular turns. The cars first arrive at the highest point, giving them a lot of potential energy.

When the cars start to descend along the rollercoaster, this energy that they have because they are very high up is converted into the energy of motion, and as a result the cars move very quickly. It carries on like this until it has finished.

4

Let the backpack go without pushing it. It is very important that you do not push it; just let it go. The backpack accelerates as it moves away from you… but then comes back toward your nose without touching it. Don't move a muscle! Do you dare?

Continue investigating

Try releasing the backpack at different heights, and pay attention to the height at which the swing arrives at when it returns. You will see that it never exceeds the height at which you let it go. But a little lower yes! What has happened to its energy? Has it been lost? No, remember the secret; it is always retained! What has happened is that it has interacted with the air, pushing it.

Hydrogen peroxide, quickly!

Don't tell me that you've fallen over in the park and cut yourself again.

Quickly! A little hydrogen peroxide to disinfect the wound! Do you know why white foam forms when you use hydrogen peroxide?

Find out why with this experiment!

Experiment

What will you need?

- Two transparent glasses
- Frozen steak
- Hydrogen peroxide
- A plate

Do you want to see how hydrogen peroxide reacts with blood?

1 Place a steak to defrost on a plate. Once it is defrosted you will see that there is reddish liquid on the plate. This is a mixture of blood and water.

2 Fill half a glass with hydrogen peroxide. A transparent glass will be much better, so that you can properly observe what happens.

3 Drain the blood from the plate into a glass to make it easier to work with.

THINK LIKE A SCIENTIST

Where is all of that foam coming from?

If you could observe normal water under a powerful microscope you would see that it is composed of tiny particles called water molecules. Hydrogen peroxide is also composed of molecules. They are almost the same as water molecules but trap oxygen. Blood contains two substances called catalase and peroxidase that react when they come into contact with hydrogen peroxide, freeing the oxygen. They transform the hydrogen peroxide into normal water and oxygen. Since this is a gas, it forms bubbles and foam as it escapes.

Hydrogen peroxide as a disinfectant

You need oxygen to breathe, but there are some living things that die if surrounded by oxygen—for example, bacteria that cause wounds to become infected. So when hydrogen peroxide is applied to a wound, the white froth, laden with oxygen, suffocates the bacteria and the wound is cleaned... if only temporarily!

To properly disinfect a wound, it must be cleaned regularly with hydrogen peroxide or other more efficient disinfecting products.

Battle first-aid kit

Soldiers who fought in World War I, a huge war fought between countries across the world at the beginning of the last century, was one of the first to use hydrogen peroxide to disinfect wounds. It was cheap and easy to manufacture and transport to the battlefield.

4

Pour the blood into the glass of hydrogen peroxide. You'll see that it produces lots of foam!

Continue investigating

With the help of an adult, hold a match closely to the foam that is formed in the glass during your experiment. You will see some small flashes! This is the oxygen inside the bubbles that you have freed in the chemical reaction! It will burn faster when you hold the flame of the match closer, producing some large flashes.

The ones that don't bite

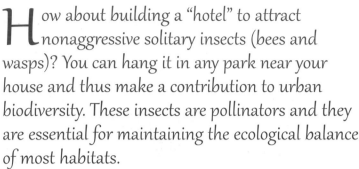

How about building a "hotel" to attract nonaggressive solitary insects (bees and wasps)? You can hang it in any park near your house and thus make a contribution to urban biodiversity. These insects are pollinators and they are essential for maintaining the ecological balance of most habitats.

What will you need?

- A perforated brick
- A hand drill or a corkscrew
- Some reeds
- Elder or bamboo twigs
- Pruning shears
- Straw
- Clay

Experiment

Would you like to convert the parks in your city into places that are filled with life, where you can look at flowers, insects, and birds and appreciate how important they are?

1

Get some reeds and cut them into sections about 8 inches (20 cm) long, trying to make sure that each section of reed has a knot (the natural division between two segments) very close to one of the ends.

8 in.

2

Do the same with any other type of available plant that is hollow inside, such as elder and bamboo; choose pieces with different diameters.

3

Using a hand drill or a corkscrew, hollow out the ends of the reeds that have no knot. Some plants do not have knots; in these cases, plug one end with clay.

THINK LIKE A SCIENTIST

Do you think it would be possible to collect honey made by this type of bee?

Do you think that by putting out these insect nests you are encouraging other animals to come?

Despite what many of us think, the bees that live in colonies, such as honeybees, are species far rarer than the number of bee species that lead solitary lives. Solitary bees lay their eggs in the soil, in little holes in rocks, or in hollow logs.

The species of solitary bees and wasps lay several eggs in the same hole, leaving a mixture of nectar and pollen next to each egg. This will be the first food for the larvae when they come out of the eggs, but they do not make honey!

By making this nest for nonsocial insects you will help enrich the biodiversity of your town or city, since facilitating their reproduction will increase their numbers, and in turn the number and variety of insect-eating birds will increase.

Bees are endangered!

Recently much has been published about the disappearance of honeybees. Scientists do not know precisely what is causing this disappearance, but it appears that the most important factor is the use of chemical pesticides, which can kill off entire colonies. Also, the proliferation of monoculture (growing just one crop) continually makes it harder for honeybees to find the flowers they need for gathering pollen. As the famous statement attributed to Einstein says, "When the bees disappear, humans will have only another four years to live."

Continue investigating

Most of the fruits that we eat depend on pollination by insects. Flowers have bright colors to attract insects. This means that insects recognize colors, something that most mammals cannot do. In exchange for nectar or a little pollen, bees help fertilize plants and allow the formation of fruits and seeds. But not all flowers are brightly colored. How do you think they are pollinated? Check it out by looking up the meaning of the word *anemophily*.

4 Get a brick of the type that has holes in it and put sections of hollowed-out reed into the empty spaces in the brick.

5 In two other empty spaces put in sections of the other plants that you have gathered (elder, bamboo, etc.).

6 In the two remaining spaces put in a little straw through one end and seal the other end with clay.

Create a fossil

Fossils are the petrified remains of living creatures (bones, shells) or traces of their activity (footprints, feces). These remains have been conserved in the strata of sedimentary rock after undergoing greater or lesser transformation. Fossils are formed when a plant, bone, or creature dies and is covered with many layers of earth. Over thousands of years of pressure on the object and after chemical transformations, it creates an impression of itself in the rock that contains it.

What will you need?

- **Plaster of Paris**
- **Water**
- **Modeling clay**
- **Vaseline**
- **Small natural objects (seashells, bones, leaves, etc.)**
- **Disposable cups**
- **Plastic spoons**
- **Newspaper or paper napkins**

Experiment

The process of fossilization is very slow and requires millions of years to pass. But we can obtain an imprint or trace of a living being that quickly creates fossils that closely resemble real fossils.

1 Choose an object with which to mold your fossil (a leaf, seashell, twig, bones…).

2 Mix the Plaster of Paris with water. Use one part Plaster of Paris to two parts water, mixing them well in a disposable cup with a plastic spoon. Leave it stand while you knead the modeling clay until it is soft and malleable.

3 Cover the object in vaseline and press it into the modeling clay to form an imprint. The object will not become stuck to the clay because of the vaseline. Carefully remove the object; you have created a mold in the shape that you have decided on.

THINK LIKE A SCIENTIST

When an organism dies, its remains quickly decompose and dissolve due to the presence of bacteria, other animals, the wind, rain, and sea waves. But if the corpse is buried in sediment soon after death, it is safe from mechanical and biological agents, greatly increasing the possibility that it can become fossilized. The process of fossilization begins when soft parts disappear and the gaps are filled in by sediment that surrounds them. At this point they begin a series of chemical transformations, little by little replacing the organic compounds of those remains with minerals.

Continue investigating

You can try another method of fossilization using dough made of sand and yeast. Make a 50/50 mixture of sand and yeast in a plastic cup. Then add water so that it is absorbed by, but does not soak, the liquid. Take a shell and gently press it on top of the dough. Cover the shell with more sand and yeast dough and add a little more water. Leave the contents of the glass to dry out for one day. When it is hard, break the disposable cup, strike the block firmly, and you will find a fossil in its mold.

Clocks from a time long ago

Some already-extinct living things were able to colonize large areas and lived brief lives. Fossils formed from this type of living beings are known as guide fossils or characteristic fossils. These fossils can be used to place rocks in a particular geological period. Furthermore, they serve to establish relative chronology between rocks. When two rocks containing fossils are compared, the oldest rock is that which contains the oldest fossil.

4 Fill the imprint of your object with Plaster of Paris. Smooth the plaster up to the level of the modeling clay, forming a flat surface. Place your clay and plaster on a newspaper and leave it to dry. You will have to wait at least overnight, but it is better to wait two or three days.

5 Remove the clay from the hardened plaster to remove the fossil. The shape of your object should be recreated in plaster with every detail intact.

Lucy, the most famous fossil in the world

On November 24, 1974, a group of investigators headed by US anthropologist Donald Johanson discovered the fossil remains of the skeleton of a female hominid approximately 20 years of age and between 3.2 and 3.5 million years old. After analyzing all of Lucy's features, it was concluded that they belonged to the species Australopithecus afarensis, and it remains to this day the oldest fossil hominid ever discovered.

Multiply your strength!

Do you think that you're not strong enough to lift an adult two hand spans off the ground? Then you are very wrong; you are perfectly able. You just need a lever, and you don't even have to build it; you've got one in the park!

Experiment

Do you want to know how you can lift someone heavier than yourself without effort?

What will you need?

- A seesaw
- An older person who weighs much more than you

1

Find a seesaw in the park—one that normally seats two children, one at each end, and requires momentum to make it move.

2

Choose an adult that you would like to surprise and ask them to sit at one end. Sit yourself at the other end. You will see that the seesaw inclines toward the adult because they weigh much more than you.

3

Now ask the adult to stand up and position themselves a little closer to the center. Try different positions until they rise up when you sit down.

THINK LIKE A SCIENTIST

How have you been able to multiply your strength?

You have transformed the seesaw into a lever: a machine that allows large weights to be lifted using a bar and a fulcrum that helps out. Normally when you use a seesaw, the fulcrum is in the middle. But the closer the person you want to lift is to the fulcrum than you, the less force is required to lift them!

Levers everywhere

Levers are everywhere. Perhaps you use them when you cut your nails (nail clippers). But here, its power is used not to lift weight but to cut something as hard as your nails, with very little effort. Ask your parents to show you a car jack! It is a small lever used to lift up a car… using only your hands! And then change the tire if it is flat.

There are other types of mechanisms that can lift heavy weights with little force: pulleys and gears. You simply pull a rope with little force to lift very heavy objects. They are used to raise and lower boats. The trick: to lift the boat a single inch, you need to pull several feet of rope!

"Give me a place to stand and with a lever I will move the whole world."

A very clever Greek named Archimedes, who lived about 2,200 years ago, was amazed at the power of the lever. It could move anything, no matter its weight, hence his famous quote.

4

When you find the correct position the seesaw is acting as a lever. You can lift the adult up just by sitting down, or even by just pushing down on the seat with your hand.

Continue investigating

Try building a lever at home with a plank of wood and another object such as a small box to act as a fulcrum. Place something heavy such as a pile of books on one end of the plank, and see how hard you have to push to lift them. Now move the fulcrum (the small box) closer to the books and see how you can lift them much more easily.

A different kind of birthday party!

This year you're going to celebrate your birthday with a party in the park, and all of your friends are invited. Of course there will be a cake, candles, and balloons. By using chemistry you can learn to inflate balloons as you have never done before and blow out the candles in an unusual way. Would you like to try this?

What will you need?

- Small water or soda bottle
- A balloon
- A glass
- White vinegar
- Baking soda
- Candles (for a birthday cake)
- Tablespoon
- An adult

Experiment

Who wants to surprise everyone by blowing up balloons and extinguishing candles without blowing?

1 Take an uninflated balloon and put three or four tablespoons of baking soda inside (whichever fits).

2 Find a small water or soda bottle and fill it about halfway with vinegar.

3 Stretch the balloon over the mouth of the bottle so that the rubber fits snugly over it, as if it were the cap.

THINK LIKE A SCIENTIST

Why has the balloon inflated without being blown into? Why have the candles gone out?

Mixing the baking soda with vinegar (acetic acid) has caused a chemical reaction that produces a gas, carbon dioxide. The carbon dioxide produced in the bottle cannot escape and rushes into the balloon, eventually inflating it.

When you cause this same reaction in a jar that is larger and has a wider aperture, the carbon dioxide can escape, but most of it does not because it is heavier than air and remains floating on the vinegar in the jar. When you incline the jar toward the candle, you are pouring carbon dioxide over it. The flame of the candle needs oxygen to continue burning, but carbon dioxide pushes away oxygen, extinguishing the candle!

Continue investigating

You can repeat the two experiments with other things that also produce a reaction, such as the calcium carbonate in a broken eggshell or crushed marble, and with other acids, such as lemon juice in place of vinegar. You can even inflate a balloon with the carbon dioxide present in yeast! Mix a couple of tablespoons of yeast and a couple of tablespoons of sugar in a bottle with hot water. Cover it with the balloon and place it in a saucepan with hot water. The yeast will inflate it by emitting carbon dioxide while the sugar is used up!

Carbon dioxide fire extinguishers

Have you noticed those red cylinders hung on garage walls? They are extinguishers that put out flames in case of a fire. Stored inside them is a gas at high pressure—carbon dioxide!

4 Shake the balloon so that all of the baking soda falls inside the bottle onto the vinegar, and... surprise! The balloon inflates without being blown up!

5 Next, take an empty glass and fill about a third of it with vinegar. Put a few tablespoons of baking soda directly on top. Observe the reaction and wait until the foam has descended a little.

6 With the help of an adult, hold the glass close to the candles and incline it slowly toward them so that the vinegar does not pour out. Just like magic, the candles go out without being blown or touched!

In search of starch

W hile walking through a park maybe you have noticed leaves with two colors, green and white. Leaves with two or more colors are called variegated. You know that the green is due to chlorophyll, which is responsible for making sugars through the process of photosynthesis; but do you want to see if the white areas also perform photosynthesis?

What will you need?

- Variegated leaves with green and white areas
- A piece of paper and pencils or markers
- A pot to boil water in
- Two plates or small trays
- 96% rubbing alcohol heated in a double boiler (get help from a grown-up)
- Iodine solution (used for disinfecting wounds)

Experiment

Plants use photosynthesis to produce sugars, which they store in the form of starch. Would you like to know how to detect the presence of starch in these leaves?

1 Select a variegated leaf; it can be from ivy, a spider plant, a ficus, an *agalaonema*, a dieffenbachia, a box elder, and others. Draw the shape of it on a piece of paper and indicate the areas of green and white.

2 Put the leaf into a pot of boiling water for about 4 or 5 minutes.

3 Put the boiled leaf on a plate and cover it with alcohol heated in a double boiler; keep it there until all the green color is gone.

THINK LIKE A SCIENTIST

What color were the previously green areas dyed?

Does this new color acknowledge the presence of starch?

When the green areas photosynthesize, they produce starch; however, the white areas cannot due to their lack of chlorophyll.

Iodine solution is a rich yellow color, but when it comes in contact with starch (and only starch), it turns a very deep violet that is sometimes so intense it seems to be black.

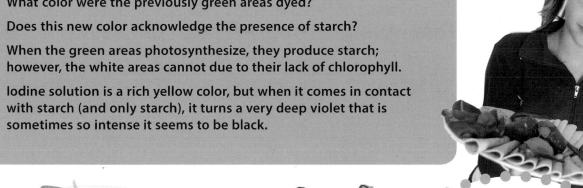

The importance of starch

Starch is the basis of human food, since the glucose that forms it is our main energy source. Starch is the main ingredient in wheat, rye, rice, corn, millet, potatoes, and tapioca.

Quality control

You can put drops of iodine on your food to test if it has starch in it. If you try this with bread or potatoes, you'll see they definitely do have starch. But you'll also find it in foods that you wouldn't expect... such as lunch meats.

8-10◊

4 Take out the leaf; put it onto another plate with water and 8–10 drops of iodine and let it sit for a couple of minutes.

5 Remove the leaf, look at its new coloration, and compare it to the drawing that you did earlier.

Modified starch

There is currently a lot of debate and news coverage about the use of genetically modified starch as food because it can cause allergies and contaminate nearby traditional and organic crops.

Foods containing genetically modified starch are as labeled as "modified starch." It is made by inserting genes from another species (such as maize) into the nucleus of the cells of the plants that produce the starch.

Shall we make a well?

Groundwater has been used by humans since antiquity through the construction of wells. Many people believe that the water from wells originates in underground lakes rather than through pores and natural fractures in the rock. To help you understand what actually happens, we are going to make a model well with materials that you can easily find at home.

What will you need?

- A pump from a bottle of liquid soap with some holes drilled in its base to prevent the pump from becoming clogged and simulating a real well
- The bottom section cut from a 2 liter, transparent soda bottle
- Thick sand or gravel
- Water in a small watering can
- A glass to recover the water

Experiment

We are going to observe how water infiltrates through pores and between grains of sedimentary rock to accumulate at the bottom of a well.

1

Take the pump from a bottle of liquid soap, insert it into the perforated pump, and place it upright in a plastic container (for example, the bottom section cut from a 2 liter, transparent soda bottle).

2

Place gravel or coarse sand around the pump until the container is almost full.

3

Imitate rainfall by pouring water over the sand until the container is about three-quarters full.

THINK LIKE A SCIENTIST

Is there an underground lake in your model? In that case, where does the water come from? You've seen that there is no lake and that the water is located in the pores between the grains of sand. What needs to be done to ensure that a well does not dry up and the water supply is maintained? In order to ensure that the well does not dry up, there must be a supply of water to the extraction zone, either directly by the infiltration of rainwater or by the underground movement of water from other more distant areas of infiltration.

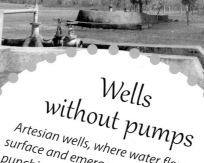

Continue investigating

Do the experiment with different types of materials (coarser, finer, or a mixture of many of them) and determine which types of soil are best for accumulating underground water that can be extracted. Note that even though the same amount of water is used, there are soils in which the tube from the well fills with water quickly and others in which this happens very slowly. Materials in the subsoil that can store water and allow for easy extraction to the surface are called aquifers.

Wells of "black gold"

Water is not the only thing that is found in wells. Many wells are built to extract oil from oil aquifers, which are geological features where oil has accumulated and remains trapped, without being able to escape through the permeable rock surrounding it. To be able to extract this oil, it is normally necessary to sink very deep wells, sometimes reaching 3 miles below the surface of the Earth.

Wells without pumps

Artesian wells, where water flows to the surface and emerges as a jet, are made by punching a hole in a confined aquifer, i.e., one that is subjected to too much pressure by the materials above and below it. When this terrain is drilled, the water rushes to the surface without the need for a pump, as does the water from a hose which has a pore or hole along its length.

4

Pump a little water from the well into a glass and observe if the level of gravel/sand has lowered.

A water volcano

Yellowstone National Park in the United States is famous for its geysers. These geysers produce eruptions of water as a result of the sudden evaporation of water through the subsoil. For this to occur there must be an increase in temperature to higher than normal at a few feet in depth. There must also be a long and narrow passage between the surface and the cavity flooded to a certain depth, and, in addition, this cavity should be constantly filled with water due to (for example) an underground network of water channels.

Pass me the ball!

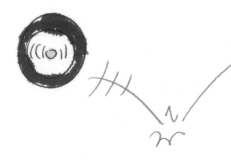

Surely you have gotten on a park merry-go-round and pushed it hard, going around and around without stopping, until you are completely dizzy.

But have you ever taken a ball with you? Try it and you will be surprised!

What will you need?

- A park merry-go-round
- Two friends
- A ball

Experiment

Do you want to see movements that are not as they seem?

1

Sit on a park merry-go-round with a ball, and ask one of your friends to sit in front of you. Ask another friend to push the merry-go-round and stay off it to observe what happens.

2

Pass the ball to the friend in front of you by rolling it along the floor of the merry-go-round. Aim well! Did it reach him/her?

3

Try several times with different angles and force, trying to get the ball to your friend and noting how the ball moves. Did it go in a straight line or a curve?

THINK LIKE A SCIENTIST

Did the ball go straight or curve around?

You and your friend who received the ball will agree: the ball "twists" as it is launched. Instead of following a straight course, it changes direction and heads away from the merry-go-round. Perhaps at some point you have made a successful pass, taking the "effect" into consideration.

But when you get off the merry-go-round there is no way that you will be in agreement. The friend who did not ride the merry-go-round is convinced that the ball traveled in a straight line. Eventually you rolled it a little to the side, but also in a straight line toward your friend.

Don't argue anymore! You all have your reasons. What happened depends on what you see when you are moving!

Continue investigating

With enough practice you will see that it is possible to throw the ball and recover it when you reach the same place in the circle. But what is a circle for you appears to be a straight line for a watching child!

4

Get off the merry-go-round and ask the friend that was watching what he/she has seen and if the ball traveled in a straight line or a curve.

Coriolis and cannons

During World War I, some soldiers fired cannons at their enemies from a boat near the Maldives. But every shot missed the enemies because the soldiers did not take the Coriolis effect into account, and all of their cannonballs ended up in the water!

Cyclones

This strange movement of the ball that you have seen was discovered in 1836 by a French scientist named Coriolis. The force that seems to twist the path of the ball is called the Coriolis effect. Do you think that once you get off the merry-go-round in the park you will not see these strange movements? You are wrong! You would have to completely leave planet Earth, which rotates constantly. This is why the great currents of air in the atmosphere are diverted to one side as your ball was, and also why tropical cyclones form in the circular swirl that you see on weather maps.

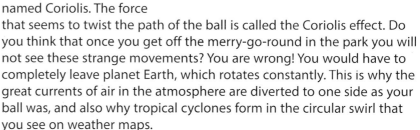

Looking for light

Plants can't see... but they can "feel" light and recognize its presence. In this experiment, which you can modify if you want, we show you how to check how skillfully plants can contort and adapt to reach the precious light.

What will you need?

- A shoe box
- Two strips of cardboard the same width and height as the inside of the box
- Adhesive tape
- Scissors
- Small glass with a thick layer of absorbent cotton soaked in water
- Two or three seeds (they can be beans)
- String

Experiment

Do you want to become an engineer-biologist and design a house maze to see how plants have the capacity to grow toward the light?

1
Find a shoe box and place the two strips of cardboard to divide the interior into two or three similar sized sections.

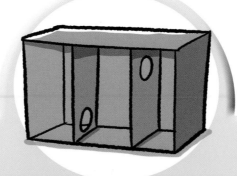

2
Make circular holes about 1 to 1.5 inches (3–4 cm) in diameter in each strip of cardboard (not aligned). Design your maze any way you want.

3
Make an opening the same size as the holes at the top of the box, which you will place vertically. This window of light should not be aligned with the holes in the strips of cardboard inside the box.

THINK LIKE A SCIENTIST

Why are the holes not aligned?

What is the mechanism that allows plants to grow toward the light?

If the holes were aligned with the top hole, when the light enters, we wouldn't be proving that the plants contort as they grow to reach that light.

Plants lean toward the light because the light reduces their cell growth. Consequently, the unlit section of the plant grows more than the lit section, directing the plant toward the light (positive phototropism).

Continue investigating

This experiment also allows us to check if a lack or excess of light determines if plants grow much taller.

You can verify this by placing another glass with seeds in the box, but this time in broad daylight next to the shoe box. Compare the results!

Cultivating asparagus

White asparagus are the largest asparagus because they are cultivated underground; growing without light, they are taller and thicker but do not produce chlorophyll.

4 Place a small glass with absorbent cotton soaked in water and two of the seeds inside at the base of the box. Put the lid on the box.

5 Close the lid securely with string or adhesive tape. Stand the box on its side in a place with lots of light and leave it for several days.

Gigantic!

In the spring of 2009 some wild asparagus gatherers found an abnormally large stalk of asparagus that was 14 feet (4.5 m) long.

Surely some of its extraordinary size was due to genetic factors, but growing in an environment without much light greatly increased the effect.

The mountain that moves

Masses of soil are often naturally displaced by excess water in the soil and the force of gravity. The trigger for these processes is normally torrential rain, since it increases destabilizing forces and reduces soil's resistance to slide. In this experiment you will build a model that will help you understand why these soil movements occur.

Experiment

What will you need?

- A transparent container (for example, an empty fish tank)
- Modeling clay
- Sand
- A protractor
- A pitcher
- Scooper bowl
- Water

What happens to the sand when you pour the water in? Does it move?

1 Create a clay slope against one wall of the container.

2 Pour sand on top of the clay until it forms a layer. You'll notice that the fine, dry sand will slide down the slope.

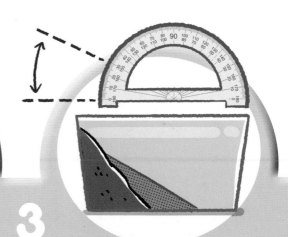

3 Measure the angle of the sand layer with the protractor.

THINK LIKE A SCIENTIST

What happened after the water was poured over the sand? Did the incline of the sand layer change? Why? You've seen that by adding water, the layer of sand is displaced, settling into a gentler slope. In this experiment you have demonstrated that landslides are conditioned by substrate material (material that forms a base). When it rains on a porous material such as sand, which lies on a waterproof material such as clay, it is soaked in water because it cannot infiltrate and begins to slip.

Continue investigating

Try the same experiment using different materials as both base and surface layers. Try a sand base and a top layer of gravel or clay, or gravel base with a top layer of sand or clay, or a gravel base with a top layer of clay. Which will be more stable? Which will hold more water without becoming unstable?

Is it really moving?

Soil movements are often very slow, so they are difficult to see unless you know what you are looking for. On a stable incline, trees and poles will be vertical. But when there is a level of instability, they tend to lean in the direction in which the hillside is moving.

4

Slowly pour water on the sand until it slides. Measure the angle of the slope again.

Fishing the earth

You've probably seen on many roads or on the slopes of inhabited areas that some hillsides are protected by metal nets anchored to the ground. These protect against small landslides and rockfalls that might fall on roads, people, or houses.

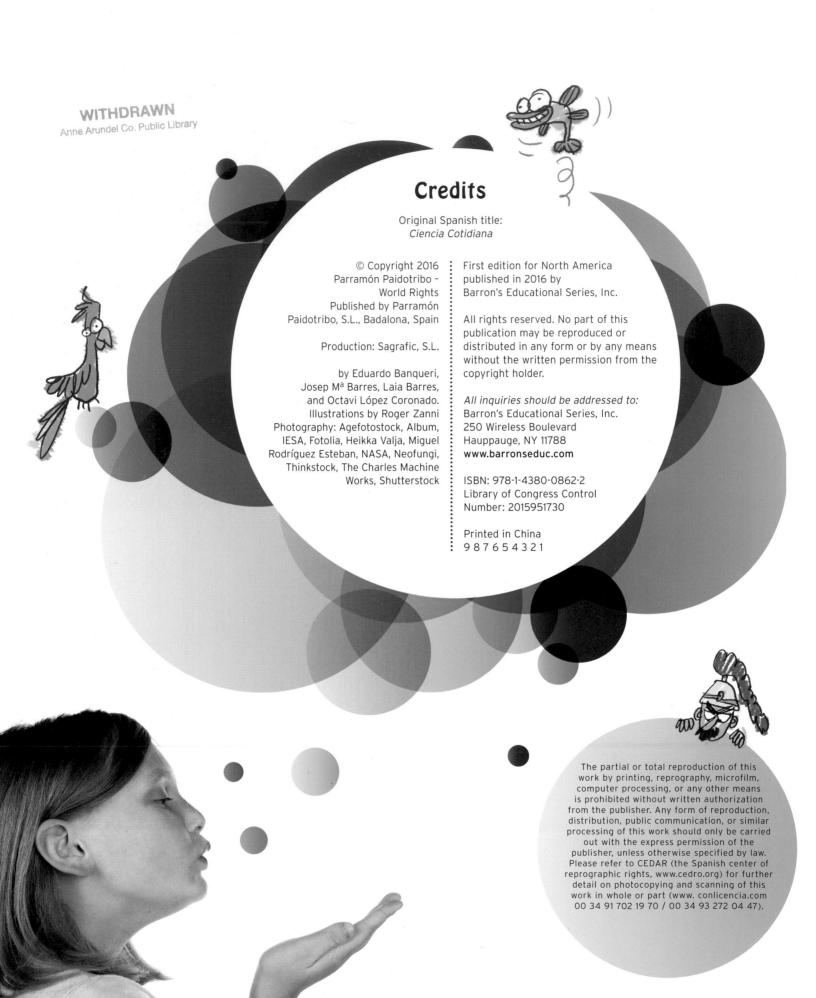

Credits

Original Spanish title:
Ciencia Cotidiana

© Copyright 2016
Parramón Paidotribo –
World Rights
Published by Parramón
Paidotribo, S.L., Badalona, Spain

Production: Sagrafic, S.L.

by Eduardo Banqueri,
Josep Mª Barres, Laia Barres,
and Octavi López Coronado.
Illustrations by Roger Zanni
Photography: Agefotostock, Album,
IESA, Fotolia, Heikka Valja, Miguel
Rodríguez Esteban, NASA, Neofungi,
Thinkstock, The Charles Machine
Works, Shutterstock

First edition for North America
published in 2016 by
Barron's Educational Series, Inc.

All inquiries should be addressed to:
Barron's Educational Series, Inc.
250 Wireless Boulevard
Hauppauge, NY 11788
www.barronseduc.com

ISBN: 978-1-4380-0862-2
Library of Congress Control
Number: 2015951730

Printed in China
9 8 7 6 5 4 3 2 1